"I Wish I Had Known That Yesterday!"

Microsoft Excel –
As Simple As It Gets

Lorraine G. Stephens

IP Liberty Publishing Group
Egg Harbor • Frederick • Raleigh

Cataloging-in-Publication Data.
    Stephens, Lorraine G.
        Microsoft Excel: as simple as it gets/Lorraine G. Stephens. -- 1st ed.
        p.cm. – (I wish I had known that yesterday!)
        Includes index.
        ISBN 1-893095-29-0

Library of Congress Control Number: 2004108768

1. Microsoft Excel.   2. Computers.   I. Title

10   9   8   7   6   5   4   3   2   1

Two statements constantly ring in my mind:

"You can do better!"
(Laura Green — My Mom)

"Ninety-nine and a half just won't do.
You've got to make a hundred."
(Eddie Green — My Dad)

It is to their memory that I deliver this small book of Excel reference materials to you, with the hope that it will help you to "do better" and to "make a hundred."

Table of Contents

Introduction

As a college student, I took a course in statistics. As I registered for the course I thought of the many things in our lives that revolve around statistics. How is the data used from the census? How do they determine how much weight a bridge can hold? Does the thickness of tunnel walls vary based on the body of water? These were burning questions in my mind, and I entered the class with enthusiasm. I was eager to learn these answers and more.

By the end of week three, however, I had developed a passionate dislike for the course. It made no sense to me! The answers to the questions did not gel in my mind – it was horrible. Then I realized what was missing. English! - Plain, Simple, Everyday English. The instructor made the assumption there was no need to explain the terms, just state the problems, and look for the answers. Chi, standard deviation, permutations and combinations, were not everyday terms to me. I was busy trying to translate his techno-babble, and he was moving on with problem resolution. Gosh, it's no wonder I disliked his course. You can probably share a similar story. Right?

Because of this frustrating collegiate experience I decided to better understand technical software information and teach others how to use it. I believed learning could be simple and enjoyable. I still have a secret desire to take another statistics course and write the "simplified" version

one of these days. A quick glance at current statistics texts tells me my inclination still has merit. Maybe one day I'll invest some time and energy in statisticsville.

Until that time, however, let me demonstrate to you how easily you can become familiar with using Excel to record information, analyze information, create charts, maintain a household inventory and more. This book has been written for your reading enjoyment as well as for instructional purposes. So sit back, relax, sip a coffee or a soft drink, let the information sink in, then try it and use it to meet your objectives.

As I was doing the research for writing this book, several people asked me to "please make formulas simple." It has been my intention to honor that request. You will notice a full chapter has been devoted to formulas – both the basic and the intermediate levels.

So hold on to your seats. We will cover topics beginning with the most basic and build until you are able to create meaningful charts, use Excel as a database, and create templates that will save you an unbelievable amount of time. There is a great deal of information covered in this very small book. However, I can assure you, just like my first book which makes Microsoft Word user friendly, this one will help you excel at Excel in less time than you think. As you find yourself using the material that we cover, give a cheer for yourself from me. OK? OK.

You will notice that there are two symbols that make it easy to spot specific types of information.

 Definitions will be listed with a light bulb.

 Notes- will be listed with a note pad.

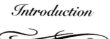

Because I believe you will find it helpful to have some sample data as you go through the examples, I have placed sample problems and data on my website for you to download. Please free to visit *www.lorrainestephens.com* to download problems and accompanying data.

Also, I have included a note area in the back of the book for you to keep note of topics that you find very helpful.

Did I hear you say you would like to contact me? Please do. I am eager to hear your comments as you immerse yourself in Excelology. Just send a note to lorraine@lorrainestephens.com.

Ready? Let's get started so you can start exclaiming:

I Wish I Had Known That Yesterday!

" Try a thing you haven't done three times.
Once, to get over the fear of doing it.
Twice, to learn how to do it.

And a third time to figure out whether
you like it or not. "

(Virgil Thomson)

What is Microsoft Excel?

A very powerful worksheet application? You bet! You can use Excel to enter any information on which you wish to perform calculations. Those calculations could be as simple as counting the names in a list, or as complex as those used determining principal and interest payments for a mortgage.

Excel is also a fantastic tool for quickly creating attractive graphs and charts. (If you are not sure what charts are, we will cover that in detail in the chapter on creating charts.) Though you might not think of Excel as a database application, it is. Since you can enter data into lists in Excel, it is a database.

DATABASE - a list or collection of related information. The phone book for Phoenix Arizona is a database. It just happens not to be electronic. Your holiday card list is a database. If you have placed it on your system it is considered an electronic database.

WORKBOOK VS. WORKSHEET

Often people are confused when trying to distinguish between an Excel workbook and an Excel worksheet. So here's the scoop! Think of a workbook as a three-ring binder. On the spine of the binder you write the name that identifies the content. Now, think of a set of tabbed dividers that you place inside. Each one of those tabs has a label that identifies the information behind it.

This is very much like Excel. The three-ring binder is the workbook. It will hold all of the separator tabs. The tabbed separators in Excel have the information written on them rather than stored behind them. Each tab should have a label, just as in your three-ring binder. The workbook will be given a name when you save it. This is the same as writing the name on the spine of your three ring binders.

> In the days of old (that means yesterday) a worksheet was called a spreadsheet

- ◆ Three-ring binder = workbook
- ◆ Each page inside = worksheet

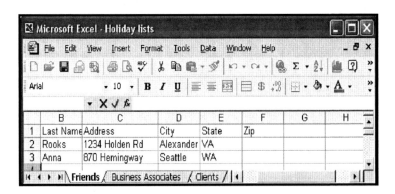

The file name for the workbook shown here is "Holiday lists." The names of the worksheets are "Friends," "Business Associates," and "Clients."

When using Excel you will want to become familiar with the layout of the window, as well as the various features that Excel offers. So let's get started.

WHAT WILL YOU SEE WHEN YOU START EXCEL?

Depending on the version of Excel that you are using, you may find a slight difference in the Excel window – but not too much. If you are still using a version of Excel that is designed for Windows 3.1, or Excel 7.0, I recommend that you stop in your tracks, go to the store, purchase a later version of Excel, install it ASAP, and throw a celebration party to mark the occasion. Now you're ready for Excel.

Let's take a look at the window for a moment. The "window" is nothing more than the area where you will manage your Excel project. The Excel picture on the following page is Excel 2000. In Excel XP there is a slight difference in the placement of some of the buttons on the toolbar. We will cover many of those. Excel XP also has a Task Pane to the right of the worksheet window. To keep life interesting we will discuss that also.

However, if you are already familiar with the Excel window feel free to skip this part.

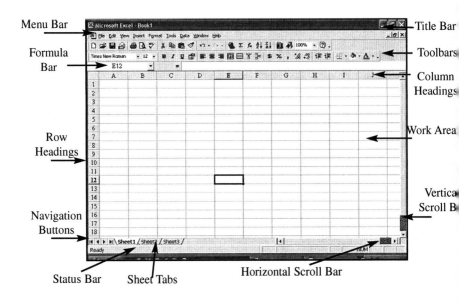

Menu Bar → | ← Title Bar
Formula Bar → | ← Toolbars
| ← Column Headings
Row Headings → | ← Work Area
| ← Vertical Scroll B
Navigation Buttons →
Status Bar — Sheet Tabs — Horizontal Scroll Bar

Like all Microsoft Office® applications, Excel has two types of windows – the application window and the file window. When you open an Excel file, the application window automatically opens. So let's take a closer look.

THE APPLICATION WINDOW

This is the window that you will see when all of the Excel files have been closed but you have not closed the application.

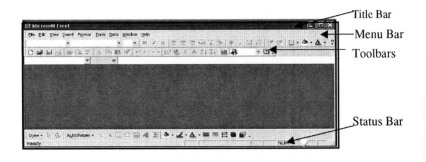

Title Bar
Menu Bar
Toolbars

Status Bar

The Task Pane in Excel XP

This was introduced with Excel XP and has many functions. Among them are:

- ◆ Accessing recently used files
- ◆ Creating files
- ◆ Opening files
- ◆ Creating files from templates
- ◆ Accessing the Excel help screens

If you select the drop-down arrow to the right of **New Work-book**, you will see that you can also use this pane to:

- ◆ Perform a search
- ◆ Insert clipart
- ◆ Paste items from your clipboard

- Viewing The Task Pane -

This task pane is found on the right side of your worksheet. If you do not see it, follow this procedure:

1. Select **View>Task Pane**.

Wasn't that neat? Now let's modify your task pane.

- Modifying Your Task Pane -

You can control how many of your most recently used files appear. The default is four. To change that:

1. Select **Tools>Options**.
2. Select the **General** tab.

3. Change the **Recently Used File List** to the number that you want to show. I normally set mine to seven or nine.

I'll bet your next question is "WHY? Why modify task pane to see more files?" The response is: "To more quickly access your recently used files. It saves you from having to find the file before opening it."

Title Bar

Every application has a bar across the top that shows the name of the application, and the name of the file. In Excel, the title bar reads **Microsoft Excel.** If you have a file open, the file name will appear in the title bar also. The temporary file name will be BOOK1, BOOK2. etc. Actually it doesn't matter what Excel calls it, because you are going to give it a meaningful name when you save it. If it is a budget file for 2006, you may name it *2006 Budget.* If it is a guest list for your daughter's wedding, you might name it *Guests For Wedding.* Once it has a name, that name will be on the title bar.

Menu Bar

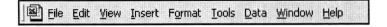

So often I hear the comment "I can't find what I am looking for without looking under each word in the menu bar." Well, don't fret if that is what's happening to you. Think of how closely this parallels a menu in a restaurant. Each restaurant has its own version of a menu. You may not be sure which items they consider pastas, appetizers, or deserts. However, once you become accustomed to the layout of the menu, your eyes naturally drift to the correct grouping. In Excel you will know that cutting, copying, pasting and deleting are *editing* features. Eventually your eyes will drift to **EDIT** on the menu bar. (I admit that some of them are not that obvious, but neither are restaurant menus the first few times you see them. Don't be reluctant to explore your menu bar. There are a gazillion features just a click away. So enjoy your cyber dining.)

Toolbars

Normally there are three toolbars showing.

◆ Standard   ◆ Formatting   ◆ Formula

As you need to perform other functions, you may choose to show other toolbars or to hide them. You will become familiar with them as you use them.

To show or hide toolbars follow these procedures.

1. Right click on any toolbar or the menu bar.
2. Click the name of the toolbar that you want to show or hide. (A check mark means that it is showing. The absence of a checkmark means that it is not showing.)

- *The Format Toolbar* -

This toolbar is used to format information. To use any of the formatting toolbar buttons:

1. Click the cell(s) that you wish to format
2. Click the appropriate button.

Remember that a drop-down arrow to the right of the button means that you have options. To see those options select the drop-down arrow, then make your choice.

Toolbar button	Meaning
Normal ▼	Chose a style to format the selected cell(s). This button may not be found on your toolbar. However it can be added if you would like to have it available. See *Customizing Toolbars* if you wish to add it.
Times New Roman ▼	Choose the desired font
12 ▼	Choose the font size
B *I* <u>U</u>	Format— Bold, Italics or Underscore
≣ ≣ ≣	Alignment—Left, center or right

Toolbar button	Meaning
▦	Merge and center—This does two things at once. It will merge all of the selected cells on that row, and centers the content of the first cell containing text into the merged cells. Here's how you do it: 1. Select all of the cells that you wish to have merged into one cell. 2. Click the **Merge and Center** button. When to use: Take a look at the worksheet below. Notice that the word "Invoice" is found in cell A1. If your desire is for "Invoice to be centered over your company name, from A1 thru C1, merge and center is a perfect option to use. With the use of **Merge and Center** we can format the title as in the worksheet shown.

Toolbar button	Meaning
	Insert Column, Insert Row: *Insert a row –* 1. Select the row number where you want your row to appear. 2. Click the **Insert Row** button When you insert a row, it adopts the formatting of the row above it. Insert a column: 1. Select the column letter where you want your column to appear. 2. Click the **Insert Column** button. When you insert a column, it adopts the formatting of the column to the left of it.
$ % ,	Format as currency, percent or commas. The comma formatting will format 1000 as 1,000.
	Increase decimals or Decrease decimals. Each time you click the Increase Decimal button you will show an additional decimal place in your cell. This does not change the internal value in the cell, simply the way that it is being displayed. The same is true for the decrease decimal button.

Toolbar button	Meaning
	Caution: If your cell value is 2.57 and you reduce the number of decimal places twice it will become 2.6 the first time, then 3.0 the second time. However inside of the system it is still stored as 2.57. That is the value that will be used in any calculations that you perform on that cell. For example: ◆ You enter 2.57 in the cell ◆ You reduce the number of decimals until the cell value is 3 ◆ You multiply the cell by 2 ◆ The answer is 5.14 not 6.0
𝄪 𝄪	Decrease indent or increase indent. Often in Excel you want to have a list that is indented. Pressing the tab key, which we are accustomed to for indenting, will take you to the next cell. The Increase Indent button is your tool for accomplishing this. Below is an example of using the indent button to emphasize the names of friends and family. You can see that each name is indented.

Friends	Birthday
L. Jackson	April
E. Reynolds	January
A. McPhee	June
T. Rooks	July

Toolbar button	Meaning
	Choose a border style for the selected cell(s). Click the drop-down arrow then make your choice. Note: The drop-down arrow that is found to the right of this icon gives you several choices for the style of border that you can apply. There are twelve options from which to choose. To use: 1. Select the cells that are to have borders. 2. Click the drop-down arrow for border selection. 3. Select the desired border option.
	Fill the cell(s) with a color. This is used for shading. To use this icon: 1. Select the cells that you want to shade. 2. Select the drop-down arrow to the right of the fill button. 3. Choose a color. 4. To remove shading, select "no fill" as your color.

Toolbar button	Meaning
	Format the text color. To use this icon: 1. Select the cells for which you want to change the text color. 2. Click the drop-down arrow to the right of the text color button. 3. Choose a color.

To see what each formatting tool bar button will do, rest your mouse pointer on the button and presto, it brings up a little box called a Tool Tip. This explains the function of the button.

> If you do not see a tool tip, your options are not set for them. Follow this procedure:
> ◆ Select Tools>Customize.
> ◆ Select Options tab.
> ◆ Put a check mark next to **Show Screen Tips on Toolbars**.
> ◆ Select OK.

The tool tip "Currency Style" appears when you rest on the $ symbol. This means that a very quick way to format a number and represent it as currency is:

1. Select the cell(s) that contain the numbers.
2. Click the $ symbol.

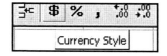

You are adding to your Excel knowledge with every click. It's fun isn't it? Let's take a look at the Standard Toolbar.

- *The Standard Toolbar* -

Along with the formatting toolbar, the standard toolbar should always show. It has icons to create a new file, save, print, etc. Though you may not see the word Standard, on the toolbar, you should still look for the icons that you see above. They identify this as the Standard Toolbar.

Toolbar button	Meaning
	New file, Open a file, Save a file. *Note:* *The white page with the turned down corner will give you a new* **workbook,** *not a new worksheet.*
	Send the file via e-mail.
	Print.
	Print Preview.
	Spell check. This will spell check your entire document – unless you have highlighted specific cells. In this case it will only spell check the cells that you have highlighted.

Toolbar button	Meaning
✂ 📋 📋	Cut, Copy, Paste. Cut will cut the data and place it in the clipboard, so that you can paste it where you want it.
🖌	Copy the format. Once you have formatted a cell you might want to use the same formatting on other cells. Rather than remembering all of the formatting attributes, simply: 1. Click in the cell that is already formatted the way you want. 2. Click the Format Painter button 3. Click in the cell(s) whose formatting you wish to change. 4. If you have several areas to change, double click the Format Painter button. Your mouse pointer will remain a paint brush until you press the **ESC** key.
↶ ▾ ↷ ▾	Undo and Redo.
🌐	Create a hyperlink. If you wish to jump to (hyperlink to) a file by clicking on the contents of a cell, create a hyperlink from that cell.
Σ	Automatically sum. This will automatically sum the numbers above or the numbers to the left of the selected cell. In Excel XP this has a drop-down arrow and provides additional functions.

Toolbar button	Meaning
![fx]	Paste a function. A method of creating formulas without having to know the exact format. (In Excel XP this button is called Insert Function and is on the formula bar).
![A↓Z Z↓A]	Sort ascending, sort descending.
![chart icon]	Create a chart or graph. This icon starts the wizard to create a chart or graph.
![100%]	Change the magnification. You can choose a magnification from the list or type in the magnification that you desire, and press the Enter key. [I do believe this could be age related. 100% once worked fine for me. Now I find myself typing in 125%.]

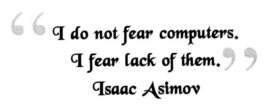

**" " I do not fear computers.
I fear lack of them. " "
Isaac Asimov**

- *Showing Additional Toolbars (or Hiding Them)* -

To show a toolbar that is not currently on the screen:

1. Right-click on the menu bar or any toolbar on the screen. Voila! This brings up a shortcut menu.
2. On the shortcut menu -notice that any toolbars that have a check mark next to them are already showing.
3. To show an additional toolbar point to the toolbar name on the shortcut menu, and click it. (It does not matter if you use the right or the left mouse button.)
4. To hide a toolbar do the same as in steps 1 and 2. Remember that a check mark means that it is showing. If it has a check and you do not want it to show, simply click on the toolbar name and it will not show anymore.

✔	Standard
✔	Formatting
	Chart
	Clipboard
	Control Toolbox
	Drawing
	External Data
	Forms
	Picture
	PivotTable
	Reviewing
	Visual Basic
	Web
	WordArt
	Customize...

Now you see it. Now you don't. As you smile at the zaniness of it all, give yourself a pat on the back. You're learning Excel shortcuts.

The Formula Bar

This bar is usually showing in Excel. The **Formula Bar** has several functions. Three of them are:

1. To show the value of what is in the selected cell. That is the **Formula Area.**
2. To tell the address of the current cell. This is found in what is called the **Name Box.**
3. To allow you to go to a cell by typing the cell address in the name box and pressing enter.

Name Box   Formula area

The formula bar above shows that the word "Kito" is in cell C4. If you wanted to go to a different cell, let's use cell M55 for our example, simply follow these steps:
1. Click in the **Name Box.**
2. Type the desired cell address.
3. Press the **Enter** key.
   Or
1. Scroll down until you see the cell.
2. Click in the cell.

You have two choices. Whichever is your preference is fine.

Status Bar

Just like the name indicates this will tell you the status of your actions in Excel. If you see:

◆ **Ready** – Excel is ready and waiting for you to enter data or formulas.

◆ **Edit** – You have double-clicked in the cell and Excel is in edit mode. When you have finished editing the cell content hit the **Enter** key or click in a different cell to deactivate edit mode. This will bring you back to **Ready** mode.

◆ **Enter** – You are typing information in a cell. To let the system know that you are finished you should press the **Enter** key or click into another cell.

◆ **NUM** – The **NumLock** key has been pressed and numeric keypad is active.

- **CAPS** – You have pressed the **Caps Lock** key. Anything that you type with your alphabet keys will be in upper case.
- **OVR** – You have pressed the **Insert** key and have placed yourself in overwrite mode. In other words, as you type new information into a cell or in the formula bar, you will delete one character for each character you type. Don't stress. Just press the Insert key again and it will toggle off.
- **SUM** or **COUNT** or **AVERAGE** or **COUNT NUMS** or **MAX** or **MIN** – This is a feature of **AutoCalculate.** You will only see this appear in the status bar if you have highlighted cells that contain some numeric data.

THE EXCEL DOCUMENT WINDOW

An Excel worksheet is made up of columns and rows. The *Columns are vertical* and the *Rows are horizontal.* In the example below we see rows 1, 2, 3, 4, 5, 6, 7, 8, 9 and 10. We see columns A, B, C, D and E. The intersection of a column and a row is called a **Cell.**

An Excel sheet is made up of cells, scrollbars, navigation buttons, and sheet tabs.

Cells

This is the intersection of a column and a row. Each cell has an address. The cell address is made up of the column letter followed by the row number. In this example the address for Kito is C4, and the address for Siti is A7.

Scroll bars

Horizontal scroll bars: When a sheet is too wide for you to see all of the information, you can scroll from left to right. To do so:

1. Place your mouse pointer on the horizontal scrollbar button.
2. Hold down the left mouse button.
3. Slide the scroll bar right or left. This will show you more of the worksheet.

Vertical scroll bars: When a worksheet is too long for you to see all of the information, you can scroll from top to bottom. To do so:

1. Place your mouse pointer on the vertical scrollbar button.
2. Hold down the left mouse button.
3. Slide the scroll bar up and down to see more of the worksheet.

Navigation buttons

When you examine the worksheet in our example you see that it has three sheets. By default they are labeled "Sheet 1", "Sheet 2" and "Sheet 3".

To select a sheet for viewing, choose one of the three options:

◆ Click on the tab that contains the sheet name (i.e. Sheet 1).
◆ Click on the proper navigation button.
◆ Right-click the navigation buttons then choose your sheet name.

Go to first sheet

Go to last sheet

Go to previous sheet

Go to next sheet

Sheet tabs – (Naming sheets)

By default Excel inserts three sheets (Sheet 1, Sheet 2 and Sheet 3) into each workbook. To make it easy for you to choose a desired sheet, give each sheet a name, and make the name relative to the information on the sheet. If you have a list of names and address for holiday greetings, you might name one of your sheets "Names and Addresses".

To name a sheet tab:
1. Double-click the sheet tab.
2. Type the sheet name in the highlighted area of the sheet tab. The name can be up to thirty-two characters long.
3. Press the **Enter** key.

ENTERING DATA IN THE WORKSHEET

Well, that is why you started this application, isn't it? You wanted to type your information into the sheet. That will be very simple.

The cell with the bold black line around it is where you going to type.
and
There will always be a cell with a black bold line around it.

The key to typing into your worksheet is:
1. Select the cell where the information or formula will appear.
2. Enter your information.
3. Press the **Enter** key to go down to the next row, or the **Tab** key to move to the next cell to the right.

Adjusting column width

Since you can adjust the column width, do not be disturbed if your data does not fit in the cell. There are three ways you can adjust the width of your column.

1. To adjust the column to automatically fit the longest existing entry:
   a. Position your mouse pointer on the line to the right of your column letter (the column separator line). Your mouse pointer will become a double headed arrow.
   b. Double-click the mouse button while resting on the line.
2. To adjust the column manually:
   a. Position your mouse pointer on the line to the right of the column letter.
   b. Hold down the left mouse button and drag the column to the desired width. (Now you are humming. Go to #3 below and let your mouse roar.)
3. To adjust the column to a specific size:
   a. Click anyplace in the column(s).
   b. Select **Format>Column>Width**.
   c. Type in the width that you want the column to be. This width represents the number of formatted characters that the  cell can contain. Do not forget that dollar signs and commas are characters.
   d. Select **OK**.

When displaying numeric data you may notice that the cell contains #######. If this happens it simply means that the column is not wide enough to hold the numeric data. Adjust the column width.

Adjusting row height

1. To adjust the row manually:
   a. Position your mouse pointer on the line below the row number in the row selector.
   b. Hold down the left mouse button and drag the row to the desired height.
2. To adjust the row to a specific size:
   a. Click any cell in the row.
   b. Select **Format> Row> Height**.
   c. Type in the height that you want the row to be.
   d. Select **OK**.

You're doing beautifully. Let's move to aligning data in a cell.

Aligning data in a cell

Unless you change the default alignment:

1. Alphanumeric information will always align itself to the left of the cell.
2. Numeric information will always align itself to the right of the cell.
3. Any information that consists of letters and numbers is alphanumeric and will align to the left.

If you wish to change this alignment, you may choose one of the methods listed.

- Toolbar method -

You may change the alignment using the toolbar buttons.

1. To align the text to the **left,** select the cell(s) and click left align button.
2. To **center** align the text, click the center align button.
3. To align the text to the **right,** click the right align button.

- Aligning data via the Format menu method -

As with any menu item, the **Format** menu item provides more options than the formatting toolbar. To align the cells: Select the cell(s) you want to align.

1. Select **Format>Cells**.
2. Select the **Alignment** tab.
3. A window like the one shown will appear.
4. To align the text horizontally within the cell, click the arrow under **Horizontal,** and select one of the options. This is a great method to use if you want your text to be at the top, the bottom or centered horizontally within the cell.

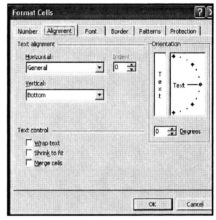

5. To align the text vertically within the cell, click the arrow under **Vertical** and choose one of the options. (Hang in there. We're almost through with this sequence.)
6. To rotate the text in the cell, rest your mouse pointer on the red dot under **Orientation**, and move it to the angle that you want the text to appear, or click the up or down arrow to change the degree angle, or click "Text" shown at the 90° angle.

Go ahead. Give it a try. You will probably say, "I can do more than what is listed in this book", and you will be right. (Raise your right hand and pledge to yourself, "I will increase my Excel knowledge and help others become more proficient as well.")

- *Text Control* -

If you can stand a little more excitement, try typing something that is just a little bit too long to fit into the cell, and then formatting it using **Shrink to fit**. Shrink to fit is great if the information is just a character or two too long. Try typing something else that is much too long then use **Wrap text**. This is good for typing a heading (i.e. Projected Start Date) where the entries under the heading really do not require a column that is very wide. The world of Excel is eager to please you.

Formatting your information

Formatting procedures for numbers, dates, or text will vary.

- *Formatting dates* -

If you type the date as 12/30/45, and you want it to appear in the worksheet as December 30, 1945, you can format your cell to show it this way. Here is how:

1. Select the cell(s) that you want to format with the month spelled out, followed by the date, and then followed by the year.

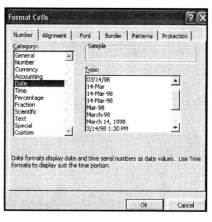

2. Select **Format>Cells**.
3. Select the **Number** tab.
4. Select **Date** in the **Category** list.
5. On the right side under **Type,** choose the format that matches the type that you want.
6. Select **OK**.

Any dates that are already typed in will reformat to the choice that you made. Isn't that neat? If you have not typed in your dates yet, they will automatically format correctly when you type them into the formatted cell(s).

- *Formatting the time to use the twelve-hour clock* -

This really is not so different from formatting dates. Sometimes you will enter a time and it will appear using the twenty-four hour clock. That is fine for military time, but the average user (myself included) will want to see the twelve-hour clock. Formatting the twelve-hour clock is not difficult at all. Follow these steps:

1. Select the cells that you want to have formatted to look like "1:00PM" instead of "13:00".
2. Select **Format>Cells**.
3. Select the **Number** tab.
4. Select **Time** from the **Category** list on the left.
5. On the right-hand side, choose the format that matches the time you want to display.
6. Select **OK**.

It's as simple as that. If you're not too tired, the answer to formatting currency and other text appears below. Grab a snack and settle in for some more fun.

- *Formatting currency* -

I encourage you to try the same steps with currency fields and number fields. Notice that you have the opportunity of indicating how many decimal places you wish to display. (Think big.) You will even be able to select the symbol you use for currency. In the USA we use the dollar symbol ($). However, since Excel can be used to represent currency in other countries you will find that you can select from several symbols by selecting the drop-down arrow next to **Symbol**.

- Formatting text -

The big question here is, "What do you want the text to look like?" Should it be bold, underlined, or italics? Do you need to indent it so that it will allow you to easily read it? Should it all fit within the cell even if it is too wide for the column? If so, how? As you can see, there are several decisions to make, and you are in control.

Let me give some very simple methods of formatting the text. I'll show you how to save some time by creating and saving a special formatting that you frequently use.

Formatting	Procedure	Shortcut
Bold	1. Select the cell(s). 2. Select **B** the format menu bar.	Ctrl+B
Italics	1. Select the cell(s). 2. Select **I** the format menu bar.	Ctrl+I
Underline	1. Select the cell(s). 2. Select **U** in the format menu bar [Note – underlining text is not the same as placing a bottom border on the cell(s)].	Ctrl+U
Indent text	1. Select the cell(s). 2. Click the indent button that is found on the Format toolbar. [To increase the indent, click the button with the arrow pointing to the right. To decrease the indent, click the button with the arrow pointing to the left.] 3. Continue to click the buttons to further increase or decrease the indent.	Increase indent: Ctrl+Alt+Tab Decrease indent: Ctrl+Alt+Shift+Tab

Formatting	Procedure
Making all of the text fit within a cell	1. Select the cell(s) 2. Select **Format>Cells**. 3. Click the **Alignment** tab. 4. Place a check mark in **Wrap Text**.
Slanted or Rotated Text	1. Select the cell(s). 2. Select **Format>Cells**. 3. Click the **Alignment** tab (as in the procedures above). 4. Increase or decrease the Degree slant by clicking the up or down arrow under **Orientation,** or by dragging the red dot under **Orientation,** clockwise or counterclockwise, to get the desired slant.

You've just earned a Ph.D. in formatting text. While you're in the formatting mood, let's explore saving your favorite formatting.

- Saving your favorite formatting: Styles -

I believe you will find the following information to be invaluable. Here's my pitch. If you happen to like a certain font, font color, border, and date format combination, you can define a **Style**. This will save time the next time you want to use the same formatting. First you must create the style. Then you can use the style.

Creating the style

1. Select **Format>Styles**.
2. Choose a style to modify. For this example we will choose Comma [0] by selecting the **Style name** drop-down arrow.
3. Place a check mark next to the formatting feature that you want to include in your style.
4. Select **Modify**.
5. Go to each tab and choose the formatting that you would like to apply to this style.
6. Select **OK**.

Using a style

1. Select the cell(s) that you wish to format using your style.
2. Select **Format>Style**.
3. Choose your style name.
4. Select **OK**.

Selecting cells

One of the biggest challenges is highlighting cells without playing the game of going down too far, up too far, or over too far. These tips will help you master selecting cells.

Objective	Action
Select one cell	1. Click anywhere in the cell.
Select a range (group) of adjacent cells	1. Click once in the first cell with the mouse. 2. Hold down the **Shift** key. 3. Click once in the last cell with the mouse.

Objective	Action
Select a range of non-adjacent cells	1. Click once in the first cell with the mouse. 2. Hold down shift key and click the last cell in the first group of cells (or drag to select the first group of cells). 3. Hold down the **Ctrl** key. 4. Select the next range. 5. Continue to hold down the **Ctrl** key as you select other ranges. 6. Release the **Ctrl** key when you are finished selecting ranges.

That sequence wasn't so bad, was it? Let's put your increased knowledge to work and find some shortcuts for entering data.

Shortcuts for entering data

Don't you love the word *Shortcut*? There are several that you can use to make your life easier when entering data. Here are three of my favorites.

- AutoComplete -

This feature is helpful because it speeds up the entry of *alphanumeric* data into *columns*. For example, if you are typing the list below, "Angel" would automatically appear once you typed "a" in cell A20.

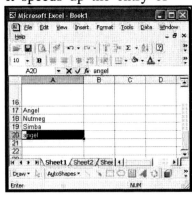

1. Type your entry into the cell.
2. Hit the **Enter** key.
3. Type your next entry into the next cell in that column.
4. Hit the **Enter** key.

5. Type the first letter of your next entry into the next cell in that column. If a cell in that column has an entry that begins with the same letter, it will automatically complete the entry.

6. If it is correct, press the **Enter** key.

7. If it is not what you desire to have in that cell just keep typing and press the **Enter** key when you have completed the cell.

8. When typing you may have to type more than one letter in order for it to complete the cell with the correct

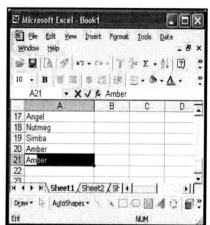

information. For example if one cell contains the text "Amber", another cell contains the text "Angel", and you want to type "Amber" in another cell in the column, you would have to type an "a" and an "m" before it would know to **AutoComplete** the cell with "Amber."

- Pick From List -

Even though **AutoComplete** is a great feature it can require that you type a great deal into the cell if you have several cells with very similar text. For example – if you have these names listed in a column:

- ◆ Learning the basics of Algebra
- ◆ Learning the basics of Gardening
- ◆ Learning the differences in insects
- ◆ Learning the differences between cutlery

You would have to type quite a bit before it knew what to automatically fill in for an entry that you wanted to repeat. This is where **Pick From List** is used. **Pick From List**, like **AutoComplete**, is used to speed up the entry of alphanumeric data into columns, because it allows you to pick one of the entries already typed rather than retyping it.

1. Right-click the cell that you want to enter the information into.
2. Select Pick From List.
3. Choose the entry that you want for that cell.

> Both AutoComplete and Pick From List require consecutive cells. If you leave a cell blank in the column list it will not work. You have to start over building the list. (Yuk!)

- Forms -

Normally when entering data you see the entire worksheet. Unless you have taken the time to make sure your column and row headings do not move you may have difficulty knowing what field you are in. (That might turn a field of dreams into a nightmare.) Using **Forms** as a data input method will eliminate that concern. It will also speed up data entry since you will not have to repeatedly move to the beginning of the row.

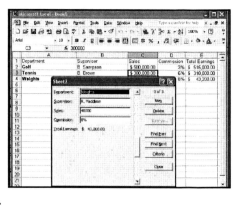

1. Enter your column headings.
2. Adjust the columns to the desired width.

3. Enter any formulas that are needed to perform calculations in the first row under the column headings and format all cells in that row.
4. Select **Data>Forms**.
5. Immediately your form will appear as the one in the picture.
6. To enter the data simply type in the form text box next to the appropriate field name.
7. Press **Tab** after each entry.
8. Press **Enter** after typing in the last field to go to the next blank form.
9. When finished entering data select **Close**. (You're done. That wasn't so bad was it?)

 Forms will work well if you have 32 fields or less.

NAMING YOUR WORKBOOK

Once you have started to create your workbook, I recommend that you save it and give it a name. In fact I would encourage you to save it frequently. Computer nerds are all in agreement that failing to save data can ruin your day. So, I repeat. Save your data often.

Rules for naming your workbook

1. File names can be up to 255 characters long. (I don't know why, but that seems to be the magic number of characters in Windows.)
2. You may use numbers, letters, blanks, or special characters.
3. Avoid using blanks as the first character.

4. Avoid using the following characters because the system reserves them for its use.

forward slash (/)	quotation marks (" ")
backslash (\)	pipe symbol (	)
greater than symbol (>)	colon (:)
less than symbol (<)	semicolon (;)
asterisk (*)	

SETTING UP A BASIC WORKSHEET

It is important that you consider the function of the worksheet in order to design it to fit your needs. Take a look at the worksheet that follows.

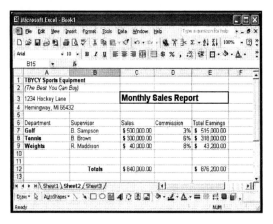

◆ The first few rows were used for identifying information.

◆ Row 6 was used for the headings. These headings identify the information that will follow.

◆ The next few rows are being used for the sales and earnings information.

◆ The totals are in row 12. (Are you with me so far? Good.)

As you set up your worksheet ask yourself the following questions:

◆ How do I want it to look when it prints?

◆ How is the information being given to me?

◆◆ If the information is coming to you with the supervisor's name first followed by the department name, you may wish to place the department name second. This will make data entry easier. You can always rearrange them if you want the department to print first. (See Sorting Horizontally in the chapter *Using Excel as a Database*.)

◆ How am I going to use the information?

◆◆ When creating a database of names and addresses that will be used for creating mailing labels, form letter or directories I recommend you have separate fields for:

First name	Second address line
Last name	City
Middle initial	State
Address	Zip

If you do not separate the fields this way it may be difficult to control the way your labels are able to print and to properly sort your information.

◆ What fields will I need in order to perform my calculations? Have I included those fields in my worksheet?

◆ Do I need to allow room for graphics? If so, where?

◆ Am I going to use Headers to identify my report?

◆ Am I going to set my worksheet up as portrait or landscape?

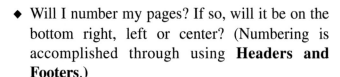

- ◆ Will I number my pages? If so, will it be on the bottom right, left or center? (Numbering is accomplished through using **Headers and Footers**.)
- ◆ Et cetera

I hope your eyes haven't glazed over with this barrage of questions. They will become habitual reminders with practice.

Once you have given some thought to these questions start laying it out. It may take a little while if you are a beginner, but it will become easier as you continue to use Excel. You may wish to refer to the chapter on Designing a Worksheet for additional consideration.

PRINTING THE WORKSHEET

If your worksheet is not a large one, printing it is quite simple. If it is a large one and will print on multiple sheets, please refer to the chapter on *Working With Large Worksheets* for additional printing tips.

Printing the entire worksheet

To print the worksheet that you are working on follow these procedures.

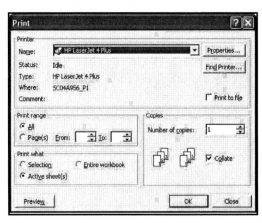

1. Select **File>Print**.
2. Choose the correct printer from the Printer list.

3. Select the pages to print from the **Print Range** section of the window.
4. Indicate the number of copies desired from the **Copies** section of the window.
5. Choose **Active Sheet(s)** from the **Print What** section.
6. Select **OK**.

Printing a portion of the worksheet

If you want to print a portion of the active worksheet follow the steps below.

1. Highlight the information that you want to print.
2. Select **File>Print**.
3. Choose the correct printer from the printer list.
4. Indicate the number of copies desired from the **Copies** section of the window.
5. Choose **Selection** from the **Print What** section.
6. Select **OK**.

By now you should have accelerated your learning curve exponentially. What's neat is once you practice these applications a few times you will become very proficient in Excelology.

Summary

In just this first chapter, we have covered many of the key points of Excel. Starting with understanding how it looks, continuing with the basics of designing a worksheet, entering data, and printing your information. Excel is a large application with many functions. *"I Wish I Had Known That Yesterday!"* is designed to deliver useful pieces of the application in a manner that will not overwhelm you.

Take a moment to view the note section in the back of the book. You may wish to keep some notes and page numbers for future reference. It's your crib sheet. Do it now. Make it a practice to record important learning points and insight for each chapter. Don't forget the data available to you on the web site. Just go to *www.lorrainestephens.com* to get the data.

Relax and enjoy the experience of *"Learning without fear."*

Customizing Toolbars

*M*ost of the buttons you will need, when first starting to use Excel, are found on your toolbars. However, as you become more adventurous and comfortable, you will want to use more and more shortcuts. I'm not kidding. Placing additional buttons on your toolbars is one way to accomplish this.

One of the features I often use in Excel is merging cells. For example, if there are five rows in a worksheet and each row contains three cells that I want to merge into one cell per row, there is not a convenient way to do this with the existing toolbars. However there is a button called **Merge Across** that will help me to accomplish this. You'll love this button. I can place the **Merge Across** button on an existing toolbar or create my own toolbar and add it, there. It's one of my favorite abracadabra buttons.

Just remember, the more buttons you add to a toolbar, the less likely it is that you will see them all without clicking the icon to display the hidden toolbar buttons.

You may choose to create new toolbars or modify an existing one. Customizing toolbars is fun. You may need to stop and get some refreshments before you continue. When you get back , we'll create a new toolbar.

CREATING A NEW TOOLBAR

1. Right-click a blank area on any toolbar.
2. Select **Customize**.
3. Select the **Toolbars** tab and click **New**.
4. Type in the name of the new toolbar (You may wish to call it **My New Toolbar**) and select **OK**.

5. To add buttons to your toolbar:
   a Select the **Commands** tab.
   b. Select a **Category** on the left side. The categories are basically the same as the menu items. If you want to add a button that will **Merge Across**, look under **Format**.
   c. Select the **Merge Across** button from the **Commands** list.
   d. Drag it up to a location on your toolbar using your mouse.
   e. Release the mouse button.
   f. If you wish to organize your icons into groups, leave a larger space between the toolbar buttons by dragging the button to the right. This will create a faint

gray line on the toolbar making the icons appear in groups.)

6. Click **Close** when you are finished adding your buttons. Good job. Now let's move on.

CUSTOMIZING EXISTING TOOLBARS

This is very much like adding buttons to your new toolbar. It's the same but different. You will get a chance to hone your mousing skills. Here's how it works.

1. Right-click a blank area on any toolbar.
2. Select **Customize**.
3. Select the **Commands** tab.

a. Select a Category on the left side. The categories are the same as the menu items. If you want to add buttons that will **Merge Across**, look under **Format**. Select the button that you wish to add to your tool bar

b. Drag it up to the location on your toolbar using your mouse.

c. Release the mouse button.

d. If you wish to create the idea of grouping, leave a larger space between the toolbar buttons. This will create a faint gray line on the toolbar making the icons appear in groups

4. Click **Close** and give your mouse a rest.

EDIT THE APPEARANCE OF A TOOLBAR BUTTON

You are free to decide how your button should look. For example you can choose whether your toolbar button should have text or an image or both.

1. Right-click a blank area on any toolbar.
2. Select **Customize**.
3. Right-click the button on the toolbar whose appearance you wish to edit.
4. From the pop-up menu choose
   a. Default style for button picture only
   b. Text Only (Always) for name of button only
   c. Image and Text for name of button and the picture of the button
5. Click **Close**.

DELETING A TOOLBAR BUTTON

1. Right-click a blank area on any toolbar.
2. Select **Customize**.
3. Click the button you no longer want on the toolbar and drag it off the toolbar.
4. Click **Close**.

A quick way of removing a button from the toolbar is to hold down the **Alt** key and drag the button off.

A speedy way to copy a toolbar button without opening the Customize Dialog Box is to hold down the **Alt** and the **Ctrl** keys while dragging the button to a new location. You would only do this if you wanted to have a button on more that one toolbar.

DELETING A TOOLBAR

1. Right-click a blank area on any toolbar.
2. Select **Customize**.
3. Select the **Toolbars** tab.
4. Select the toolbar you want to delete.
5. Click the **Delete** button found on the right side of the dialog box.
6. Click **Close**.

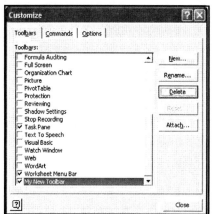

Never again worry about not having quick ways of accomplishing your tasks. You can create as many toolbars as you like and place whatever functions you desire on those toolbars. That's why the computer software gurus get the big bucks. They create cyber solutions to application problems, and put you in charge by programming in shortcuts and user-friendly procedures. If you are especially clever, you can invent your own formula for success in Excel.

Speaking of formulas (application formulas, that is) you'll be pleased to discover I have taken the mystery out of formulas in the next chapter. So if you are not too tired and have the time, I invite you to learn how to master formulas.

No More Mysteries About Formulas

$\mathcal{W}$hen I mentioned to one of my clients that I was preparing to write the Excel version of *I Wish I Had Known That Yesterday!*, he said, "Please include a chapter on formulas – and make them simple!" Thus, my goal for this chapter is to make formulas simple. There is so much to say about formulas, that even this lengthy chapter only scratches the surface. However, I can assure you that you will feel like a champion when you learn what this chapter has to offer. If you need more information on formulas, please contact me at lorraine@lorrainestephens.com.

Actually, formulas are simply small instructions to Excel telling it how to handle data, or asking it to examine data and return an answer to you. To accomplish these tasks formulas make use of:

1. The equal sign "="   4. Functions
2. Constants   5. Order of operations
3. Operators

Together these five things make up any formula you will ever use. What we will examine are some of those operators, functions and the proper format for putting them into a formula for Excel to deliver an answer. Formulas aren't as complicated as you think.

Formulas often address a range of cells. You see this often when you are using functions.

> Range – This is used to refer to a group of cells. If you highlight A1 to D8 you have highlighted the range A1:D8.

We won't attempt to cover all of the operators and functions (there's over a gazillion) but we will cover many of the commonly used ones, and several really handy ones that might be new to you. Once you are clear on the job of a particular function, and know how to word your request for Excel to deliver the correct answer, you will be surprised at how comfortable you will become with formulas. I promise. So, if you're ready to master formulas, let's get started.

STRUCTURE OF FORMULAS

The successful use of formulas always involves these two requirements:

1. Formulas always begin with an equal sign. This is without exception.
2. Formulas are typed in the cell where the results (answer) should appear.

Here are some examples of formulas:

=A1+B2+B5	Adds the value of cells A1, B2, and B5
=SUM(A6:D3)	Adds the values starting in cell A6 and ending in cell D3
=G2	Sets the value of the cell containing the formula to the value found in cell G2
=Average (A6:D8) + Sum (B12:D14) - 35	This formula will do four things. 1. It will find the average of the values in cells A6 to D8. 2. Then find the sum of the values found in cells B12 to D14. 3. Add those together. 4. Subtract 35 from the total.
=Max (B15:C33)	Finds the highest number in the cells B15 to C33.
=3* (Sum(A1:B5) +15) – Max(B15:B22) Order of operations and parentheses played an important role in this formula.	This formula will do several things. 1. It will find the sum of the cells from A1 to B5. 2. Then add 15 to that number. 3. Next it will multiply the result of these two numbers added together by 3. 4. Next it will find the highest number from B15 to B22. 5. Then subtract that highest number from the results calculated in steps 1 to 3.

I've given you six really great formulas and described their actions. None of them are complicated. Right? Notice how each formula consists of an equal sign, the necessary operators or functions, and, where necessary, parenthesis to determine the order in which these calculations would take place. Are you with me? Okay, let's move on.

 It is OK to use spaces in your formulas. It makes them easier to read and does not have an impact on the calculations.

WHAT ARE OPERATORS?

Operators tell the type of calculation you want to perform. Microsoft Excel has four different types of calculation operators: arithmetic, comparison, text, and reference.

Arithmetic operators

+ (plus sign)	Addition (8+8)	/ (forward slash)	Division (8/15)
– (minus sign)	Subtraction (8-5) Or Negation (-8)	% (percent sign)	Percent (31%)
* (asterisk)	Multiplication (8*15)	^ (caret)	Exponentiation (8^4)

Comparison operators

Operators	Example
= (equal to)	(G2=H3)
> (greater than)	(G2>H3)
< (less than)	(G2<H3)
>= (greater than or equal to)	(G2>=H3)
<= (less than or equal to)	(G2<=H3)
<> (not equal to)	(G2<>H3)

Text operator

& (ampersand)	Joins, connects, or concatenates, values in multiple cells to produce one continuous text value. ("School " & "District " & "County ", or A1& A2& A3).
	If you use an & to join fields, you often need to build in spaces between those fields. This is done by placing a space within quotes.

Reference operator

: (colon)	**Range operator**. Creates a single reference to the cells between two reference points. (A3:G2)
, (comma)	**Union operator**. Combines multiple references into one reference. (AVERAGE(A5:A20,E25:J35))

USING ARITHMETIC OPERATORS IN FORMULAS

Below are some examples of using arithmetic operators in formulas.

Formula	Operation
=A1+B3+C5	Adds the contents of whatever is in cells A1, B3, and C5
=D5/4	Divides the contents of cell D5 by 4
=C5-H2	Subtracts the value in cell H2 from the value in cell C5
=5*A2	Multiplies the value in cell A2 by 5
=6^3	Multiplies 6 by itself three times (Raises 6 to a power of 3)

COMPARISON, TEXT AND REFERENCE OPERATORS

These are used in conjunction with formulas which contain functions, and operators. Look for them when we cover the list of functions.

ORDER OF OPERATIONS

Before we discuss functions, let's clarify any blurred vision surrounding the term "order of operations". Simply stated it means "This is the order in which the operations stated in a formula will take place." You cannot change the natural order of operations — it has been in existence ever since some brilliant mathematicians noted it years ago. However, you can control it based on your knowledge of how it works and the use of parenthesis.

This is the sequence for the Order of Operations.

1. Everything in **P**arentheses takes place first.
2. All **E**xponentiations are calculated next.
3. **D**ivision and **M**ultiplication are calculated next. If multiplication and division appear in the same formula, they are evaluated from left to right as they appear in the formula.
4. **A**ddition and **S**ubtraction take place next. When addition and subtraction appear in the same formula, they are evaluated from left to right as they appear in the formula.

(**P**arenthesis, **E**xponentiation, **D**ivision, **M**ultiplication, **A**ddition, **S**ubtraction)

 Want an easy way to remember the Order of operations? Try this:

Play **E**very **D**ay, **M**ake **A S**plash.

[My thanks to Lois for this idea.]

Now let's put those rules into practice to determine the answers to the following examples.

Example	Write your answer here	Correct answer
=7*5+3*(8-2)		53
=7*(5+3*8-2)		189
=7*(5+3)*(8-2)		336
=7*5/3*(8-2)		70

If you did not get the same answers, you have neglected to drink the amount of coffee you're entitled to by now. Seriously though, review your steps to find where you might have missed one. If your answers are the same, you have an understanding of Order of Operations. *Congratulations!!!*

COMMON FORMULA ERRORS TO AVOID

Be careful when entering formulas and try to avoid these common errors:

Formula Entered	Error	Solution
=5B	Incorrect cell reference	=B5
=8*+15	Two mathematical operators are next to each other	=8*15 or =8+15
=9X12	X used instead of * as the symbol for multiplication	=9*12
=A1+5(D1/53)	missing mathematical operator	=A1+5*(D1/53)

Because the computer gurus are good at what they do, Excel will try to correct your formula if it is entered incorrectly. In Excel 2000:

◆ You receive a warning like the one below indicating the formula is incorrect.

◆ A corrected version is suggested.

◆ You are given the opportunity to accept the suggested correction or to reject it and type in the correct formula yourself.

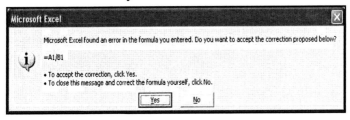

In Excel XP it will often correct the error without giving you an error message. It's nice to have a silent partner like that isn't it? And one so methodically obedient. However, if it cannot guess what you meant, a message will be displayed.

FUNCTIONS

To make functions relative to the task you are approaching, Excel, in its infinite wisdom, divides functions into categories. Those categories are:

◆ Database   ◆ Logical
◆ Date and Time   ◆ Lookup and Reference
◆ External   ◆ Math and Trig
◆ Engineering   ◆ Statistical
◆ Financial   ◆ Text
◆ Information

All of these functions can be studied by looking at the Excel help screens, which was my resource for this section. We will examine some of them. Don't worry about trying to memorize them. Excel can always show you a list of functions and tell you what they do.

> Function categories may vary depending on your version of Excel and what Add-Ins have been installed.
>
> Functions are not case sensitive.
> =SUM(A2:A5) is calculated the same as =sum(a2:a5)

View the list of functions - Excel 2000

1. Select the **Paste Function** button found on the standard toolbar. *fx*
2. Select **All** on the left side under **Function Category** to see all of the functions. Or, select a **Category** and see the functions which are associated with the category. (That's all there is to it. You're just viewed the list of functions in Excel in three easy clicks.)
3. Select **Cancel**.

View the list of functions – Excel XP

1. Click the **Insert Function** button found in the formula bar. *fx*
2. In the **Insert Function** dialog box select **All** from the **Categories** box.
3. You will see every function in Excel.
4. Select a category from the **Categories** box. You will see all of the functions in that category. (Some clever computer engineer figured out how to program that.)
5. Select **Cancel**.

Now let's take a peek at math and trig functions.

Math and Trig functions

The functions in this section can be very helpful when performing math or trig calculations. This is not a full list, but does contain some of the ones which I have found most useful.

- Creating combinations -

COMBIN(*number,number_chosen*) **Example:**

◆ Number— the number of items to choose from. ◆ Number_chosen— the number of items in each combination	How many different 8-person committees can be formed from the nine people available? =COMBIN(9,8) The answer is 9

- Raising numbers to a power -

POWER(*number,power*) **Example:**

◆ Number — the number you want to raise to a power.	◆ Power — the exponent to which the number is raised. =POWER(3,4) =3*3*3*3=81

- Find the Roman number equivalent -

ROMAN(*number*) **Example:**

◆ Number — can be a number that you type in or a reference to a cell.	=ROMAN(55) Returns a value of LV

Or you can use it as noted below:

	A
1	**Chapter #**
2	43
3	=ROMAN(A2) Returns a value of XLIII

- *Rounding numbers* -

ROUND(number,num_digits)

♦ Number — the number you want to round. It can be a number that you enter or, a cell reference.

♦ Num_digits —specifies the number of digits to which you want to round the number.

Examples:

	A
1	**45.917**
2	=ROUND(A1,0) Returns a value of 46
3	=ROUND(A1,1) Returns a value of 45.9
4	=ROUND (A1,2) Returns a value of 45.92

- *Add numbers* -

SUM(*number1,number2, ..number 30*)

♦ Number1, number2, ... are numbers or cell references that you want to total. You can sum up to 30 numbers.

Use the data in this worksheet for the examples shown:

	A	B	C
1	**Game**	**Runs batted in**	**Errors**
2	1	9	5
3	2	4	3
4	3	6	6
5	5	10	4

=SUM(4,7)
Add 4 and 7
(Answer is 11)

=SUM (B2:B5)
Add contents of cells B2 through B5
(Answer is 29)

=SUM(C2:C5,8)
Adds the values in cells C2 through C5 plus 8
(Answer is 26)

- *Add cells based on a condition* -

SUMIF*(range,criteria,sum_range)*

- ◆ Range — the range of cells you want evaluated.
- ◆ Criteria — the criteria in the form of a number, expression, or text that defines which cells will be added.
- ◆ Sum_range — the actual cells to sum.

Example:

Add up value of the prizes given to all who scored over 84 on their test.

	A	B
1	**Grades**	**Prize Value**
2	90	9
3	85	4
4	73	6
5	97	10
6		=SUMIF(A2:A5,">84",B2:B5) The answer is 23

Easy as riding in on a wave, isn't it? Let's push the envelope a little, and add a few more functions. Check out the date and time functions which follow.

Date and Time Functions

- Count the number of workdays between two dates -
NETWORKDAYS*(start_date,end_date,holidays)*

Be sure not to enter dates as text. This will cause your computer to melt down and turn into a bowl of jelly. I'm just kidding, of course. But you do not want to enter dates as text. Just trust me on this one. .

- ◆ Start_date — a date that represents the start date.
- ◆ End_date — a date that represents the end date.
- ◆ Holidays — an optional range of one or more dates to exclude from the working calendar.

Example: Using the data found in rows 1 through 5, calculate the values for rows 10 through 12.

	A	B
1	**Date**	**Description**
2	1/5/2005	Start date of project
3	3/21/2006	End date of project
4	11/8/2005	Holiday
5	11/15/2005	Holiday
6	12/1/2005	Holiday
7	1/9/2006	Holiday
8		
9		
10	=NETWORKDAYS(A2,A3) Answer is 315	Number of workdays. No holidays considered.
11	=NETWORKDAYS(A2,A3,A4) Answer is 314	Number of workdays, one holiday considered.
12	=NETWORKDAYS(A2,A3,A4:A7) Answer is 311	Number of workdays, all holidays considered.

Logical Functions
- Test a number and display a message based on results-

IF(*logical_test,value_if_true,value_if_false*)

- ◆ Logical_test — any value or expression that can be evaluated to TRUE or FALSE.
- ◆ Value_if_true — what to do if the logical test is true.
- ◆ Value_if_false —what to do if the logical test is not true.

 When reading this statement, read the first commas as "Then", and read the second commas as "Otherwise".
If the test that I make is true then do this, otherwise, do that. (Makes perfect sense, right?)

Example: This is a very useful function. Don't let the tricky parenthesis, and number of commas, defeat you. Once you master the **IF Statement**, you will use it often.

	A	B
1	**Score**	**Prize?**
2	90	=IF(A2>=84,"Congratulations","More Study Required") If the contents of cell A2 is equal to or greater 84 then write Congratulations in this cell, otherwise write Study Required. (The result is Congratulations)
3	85	=IF(A3>=84,"Congratulations","More Study Required") If the contents of cell A3is equal to or greater 84 then write Congratulations in this cell, otherwise write Study Required. (The result is Congratulations)
4	73	=IF(A4>=84,"Congratulations","More Study Required") If the contents of cell A4 is equal to or greater 84 then write Congratulations in this cell, otherwise write Study Required. (The result is More Study Required)

Nested IF statements
Sometimes it is not as simple as, do this if the statement is true or do this is it is not true. There are often several tests that have to be made to determine the value for a cell, and what actions need to be taken.

Example: Use the worksheet below.

Let's think of school grades
with this grading scheme ⟶

91-100 = A
81-90 = B
71-80 = C
65-70 = D
Below 65 = F

	A	B	C
1	Score	Prize?	Grade
2	90	Congratulations	A
3	85	Congratulations	B
4	73	More Study Required	C
5	70	More Study Required	D
6	63	More Study Required	F

The formula entered into C2 is:
=IF(A2>=90,"A",IF(A2>=81,"B",IF(A2>=71,"C",IF(A2>=65,"D","F"))))

You can have up to seven IF statements nested together.
    In this example, several logical tests have to be made to determine the outcome. This statement is read:
  ◆ If A2 is greater than or equal to 90 put an A in this cell,
  ◆ if it is not, test to see if A2 is greater than or equal to 81, if it is put a "B" in the cell,
  ◆ if it is not, test to see if A2 is greater than or equal to 71, if it is put a "C" in the cell,
  ◆ if it is not, test to see if A2 is greater than or equal to 65, if it is put a "D" in the cell,
  ◆ if none of the above are true, then put an "F" in the cell.

I know this process was a bit laborious, but once you become more familiar with nested if statements, as well as the other formulas introduced here, you'll want to use them often. Now hold on to your seat. We are going to take a look at statistical functions.

Statistical Functions

- Find the average of a group of numbers -
AVERAGE(number1,number2,..number30)

◆ Number1, number2, .. – You can list up to 30 numbers or ranges that you want to include in the calculation.

Why 30? I have no idea. Maybe the software programmers thought it would be a nice round number.

Example: Using the chart to the right, find the average salary of everyone in the sales department.

=AVERAGE (B2:B4) = 71,000

	A	B
1	Department	Salary
2	Sales	55,000
3	Sales	85,000
4	Sales	73,000
5	Support	70,000
6	Support	63,000

- Finding the number in the middle and the number most frequently used -
MEDIAN(number1,number2,...number30)

◆ Number1, number2,..- Once again, you can list up to 30 numbers from which the median will be chosen.

The median is the number in the middle of a sorted set of numbers; that is, half the numbers have values that are greater than the median, and half have values that are less. (Makes perfect mathematical sense, right?)

MODE(*number1,number2,..number30*)
- ◆ The Mode is the most frequently occurring, or repetitive, value in range of data.

	A
1	**Salary**
2	55,000
3	55,000
4	70,000
5	73,000
6	85,000

=MEDIAN(A2:A6) = 70,000

=MODE(A2:A6) = 55,000

Let's get into some really interesting areas and explore COUNTIF functions. You may want to take a stretch break first. You've been working really hard.

- Find a count based on conditions -
COUNTIF(*range,criteria*)
- ◆ Range — the first and last cells from which you want to count cells.
- ◆ Criteria — a number, test, or an expression that defines which cells will be counted.

Example:
1. Count the number of members that have the last name of Wise.
2. Count the number of members that are equal to or older than 27.

	A	B
1	Brown	43
2	Green	17
3	Wise	51
4	Stephens	25
5	=COUNTIF(A1:A4,"Wise")	=COUNTIF(B1:B4,">=27")
	The answer is 1	The answer is 2

You may want to read those explanations one more time. Okay?

I do believe you have the idea now about how the formulas are created. Let me just list a few more without going through examples.

- Counting the numeric entries in a list -
COUNT*(starting_cell:ending_cell)*

- Count the number of cells that are not empty -
COUNTA*(starting_cell:ending_cell)*

- Find the largest number -
MAX*(number1,number2,..number30)*

- Find the smallest number -
MIN*(number1,number2,..number30)*

Database Functions

Database functions are very much like the statistical functions that we have examined so they will ring familiar to you. Since we have a full chapter on *Using Excel as a Database*, I will simply list the functions here and demonstrate many of them in that chapter. They are powerful functions, so once you've glanced at the ones outlined here please go to that chapter and look at the examples, while the concept is still fresh in your mind.

- Find the average of a selected field in a database -
DAVERAGE*(database,field,criteria)*

*- Count the cells that contain numbers matching
a certain criteria -*
DCOUNT*(database,field,criteria)*

*- Find the highest number in the selected field
in a database -*
DMAX*(database,field,criteria)*

- Find the lowest number in the selected field in a database -

DMIN*(database,field,criteria)*

- Find the sum of the numbers in the selected field in a database -

DSUM*(database,field,criteria)*

Text Functions

- Join several text items together -

CONCATENATE*(text1,text2,..text30)*

◆ Text1, text2, ...You can concatenate (that's Excel techno-babble for "put together") up to 30 text items. This is very much like the text operator Ampersand (&).

Example:

	A	B	C
1	First Name	Last Name	City
2	Carolyn	Goode	Raleigh
3	Isaiah	Stephens	Yonkers
4	Tiffany	Green	Queens
5	Eddie	Stephens	Phoenix
6	Laura	Brown	Atlanta

=CONCATENATE(A2," " ,B2)
The result is Carolyn Goode
(Notice that a space had to be inserted between the two fields.

=CONCATENATE (A2," ",B2," is living in ",C2)
The results is:
Carolyn Goode is living in Raleigh.
(Notice that spaces are built into the statement "is living in".)

- *Get rid of extra spaces in a field* -

TRIM*(text)*

Removes all spaces from text except for single spaces between words. This is such a helpful function to use on text that you have received from another application that may have irregular spacing.

	A	B
1	students	
2	teachers	
3	schools	
4	school bus	
5		

1. Click cell B1.
2. Type =TRIM(A1). Press **Enter**.
3. Copy the formula from B1 to B4.

This will place the values into column B without the spaces. To replace the cells in column A with the data stripped of spaces, follow this procedure:

- ◆ Highlight B1:B4.
- ◆ Right-click and choose **Copy**.
- ◆ Right-click in A1 and choose **Paste Special**.
- ◆ Under **Paste** options select **Values**.
- ◆ Select **OK**. (I wish we could trim away those extra pounds this easily.)

How are you doing? If you are ready, we will move on as we continue taking the mystery out and putting more fun into formulas.

ENTERING FORMULAS INTO A WORKSHEET

Entering the formulas is very important. Knowing the format and knowing where you want your answers to appear are key items. It's like anything else in life: knowing what you want and where you're going is half the journey. The same goes for entering formulas. Remember, your answer will appear in the cell that contains the formula.

1. Click inside of the cell where the answer will appear.
2. Type an equal sign =
3. If using a function, type the function name and the proper format for using that function. If using operators type the proper operators.
4. Press **Enter**.

Examples – Using functions

Refer to the worksheet below for all of the examples that follow unless directed to use other data. The formulas are shown in the worksheet.

	A	B	C	D	E
1	Name	Score – Game 1	Score- Game 2	Total	Average
2	Rooks	13	21	=SUM(B2:C2)	=AVERAGE(B2:C2)
3	Givan	20	18		
4	Stephens	15	17		
5	Warrior	18	19		
6	Carter	10			
7	Total Scored	=SUM(B2:B6)			
8	Average per game	=AVERAGE(B2:B6)			
9	Average combined score of games 1 and 2	=AVERAGE(B2:C6)			
10	Average combines score for Rooks and Warrior for games 1 and 2	=AVERAGE(B2:C2,B5:C5)			
11	Highest score between both games	=MAX(B2:C6)			
12	Number of players who scored per game		=COUNT(C2:C11)		
13	Number of players who scored over 18 points in game 1. >18 points in game 2.	=COUNTIF(B2:B6,">18")			

Let's have some fun with the game scores. I'll do what I can to help you stay on track. Just follow the easy steps below.

Calculate the average score for Rooks. Place the results in E2.
1. Click in E2.
2. Type **=AVERAGE(B2:C2)**.
3. Press **Enter**.

Find the average score for game 1. Place the results in B8.
1. Click in B8.
2. Type **=AVERAGE(B2:B6)**.
3. Press **Enter**.

Find the combined average for points scored in both games. Put the results in Cell B9.
1. Click in B9.
2. Type **=AVERAGE(B2:C6)**.
3. Press **Enter**.

Find the combined average for Rooks and Warrior for both games. Place the results in B10.
1. Click in B10.
2. Type **=AVERAGE(B2:C2,B5:C5)**.
3. Press **Enter**.

Find the sum of points scored during game 1. Place the results in B7.
1. Click in B7.
2. Type **=SUM(B2:B6)**.
3. Press **Enter**.

When we study AutoSum, you will probably prefer that method for calculating the sum of consecutive numbers.

Find the highest score between both games. Place the results in B11.
1. Click in B11.
2. Type **=MAX(B2:C6)**
3. Press **Enter**.

> You can let Excel highlight the range for you. Rather than type B2:C6 use the mouse/keyboard selection method:
> 1. Click in cell B2 with the mouse.
> 2. Hold the **Shift** key.
> 3. Click in Cell C6 with the mouse.
> 4. Notice that the formula bar has the range filled in.

Comfortable? Let's keep our momentum and move on to the AutoSum button.

Using AutoSUM

- AutoSUM Button -

A shortcut way to perform the SUM function is to use the AutoSUM button on the standard toolbar. The AutoSUM button is best used when you need to add a row or a column of adjacent numbers.

AutoSum will add the numbers above the selected cell, or the numbers to the left of the selected cell. If there are numbers both to the left and above, AutoSum will add the numbers above the selected cell. (Don't you just love it? In its little electronic head, your computer partners with Excel to make your life easier.)
1. Click once in the cell where your sum is to be placed.
2. Double-click the **AutoSUM** button.

Example – Use AutoSUM to Sum (Excel 2000)

Calculate the total number (**SUM**) of points scored by Rooks in both games using **AutoSUM**. Place the results in D2.

1. Click once in cell **D2**, where the SUM will be calculated.
2. Double-click the **AutoSUM** button.

In Excel XP the AutoSUM button includes an arrow to its right which allows you quick access to other frequently used functions such as AVERAGE, COUNT, MIN and MAX. (Believe me, this is a nice feature.)

1. `Click once in the cell where the answer will be calculated.
2. Click the dropdown arrow on the **AutoSUM** button.
3. Click the function that you want to use.
4. Press **Enter**.

Example – Use AutoSum to Count (Excel XP)

Count the number of people that scored in Game 2. Place the result in C12.

1. Click in C12.
2. Click the drop-down arrow on the AutoSum button.
3. Select **Count**.
4. A marquis (I call them marching ants) will go around the cells that it is getting ready to count.
5. Press **Enter**.

Formula Pallet – Another way to enter formulas

Right about now, you are asking, "Why do I need so many options to enter formulas?" Good question. The best answer I can offer is, "Choices and preferences." Once you become

comfortable with formulas you will also discover that you have developed a preference of one method over another.

One exquisite feature of the **Formula Pallet** is the way it guides you through the steps required for each function. In the versions that follow 2000, the formula pallet even let's you ask it to suggest what function you will need to accomplish your tasks. Let's find out how exquisite it is by activating the formula pallet.

⁃ *Activating the formula pallet in Excel 2000* ⁃

1. Select the **Paste Function** icon in the [fx] standard toolbar.
2. Select the function category from the left side of the Paste Function dialog box.
3. Select the function that you wish to choose from the right side of the dialog box. Notice that a description of the function is shown below.
4. Select **OK**.
5. Depending on the function that you have chosen, the next dialog box will vary. It will let you know how many fields you must fill in to get your answer.
6. Once all of the fields are filled in click **OK**.

Example –Counting based on a condition

Use the formula pallet to count the players that scored over eighteen points in Game 1. We will use the **Countif** function. Place the results in B13.

1. Click in cell B13.
2. Click the **Paste Function** icon.   [fx]
3. If you recall that **Countif** is in the statistical category, select **Statistical** from the left side. If you do not recall the category, select **All** on the category side.

4. Select **Countif** from the right side. (Are you still with me?)
5. Select **OK**.
6. In the **Countif** dialog box, click in the **Range** text box. This is where you will enter the

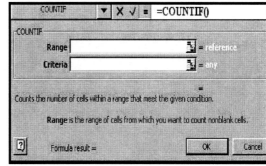

range (address) of the data that you want to test.
7. Click the red arrow in this text box to collapse the dialog box in order to see your data. (If you wish you can move the dialog box over so that you can highlight the data rather than collapsing it.)
8. Highlight cells **B2:B6** and click the red arrow to expand the dialog box.
9. Click in the **Criteria** text box.
10. Type **>18**.
11. Press **OK**.
12. The formula that will appear in the formula bar for cell B13 is:

=COUNTIF(B2:B6,">18").

- Activating the formula pallet in Excel XP -

1. Select the **Insert Function** icon in the formula bar. fx
2. Ask Excel for help by typing your question in the **Search for a function** text box.
3. Press **Enter**.
4. Select the function that you wish to choose from the recommended functions listed at the bottom.
5. Select **OK**.

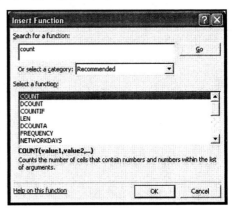

Example –Counting based on a condition – Excel XP

Use the formula pallet to count the players that scored over eighteen points in Game 1. We will use the **Countif** function. Place the results in B13.

1. Click in cell B13.
2. Click the **Insert Function** icon. fx
3. Type "**Count**" in the **Search for a function** text box.
4. Hit **Enter**.
5. Select **Countif** from the **Select a function** box.
6. Select **OK**.
7. In the **Countif** dialog box, click in the **Value1** text box. This is where you will enter the range (address) of the data that you want to test.
8. Click the red arrow in this text box to collapse the dialog box in order to see your data.
9. Highlight cells **B2:B6** and click the red arrow to expand the dialog box.
10. Click in the **Value2** text box.

11. Type **>18**.
12. Press **OK**.
13. The formula that will appear in the formula bar for cell B13 is:

    =COUNTIF(B2:B6,">18").

COPYING FORMULAS IN YOUR WORKSHEET

Refer to the worksheet we have been using. The shaded areas indicate cells that would have information copied into them.

Wouldn't it be time consuming if you had to enter the formula for every row and every column in your worksheet? Don't worry – Excel would not impose that upon you. Actually, once you enter most formulas, you can copy it to similar rows or similar columns. Love it! As we look at our worksheet, we see that several cells can have information copied into them.

The reason that copying the formulas works is because copying is relative. Since copying is relative, the formula will adjust to the row or column where it is copied. (Obedient things, aren't they?) Let's first look at how to copy a formula, then look at how the formula copies.

How to copy a formula

1. Click in the cell that contains the formula you want to copy.
2. Rest your mouse pointer on the fill handle. The **Fill Handle** is a small box in the lower right corner of the cell. Your mouse pointer will become a thin black cross when you rest on it.

3. Hold down your mouse button and drag the **Fill Handle**, in the direction that you wish to copy the formula.
4. Release the mouse button after you have copied the formula to the desired cells.
5. Your values now appear in your pasted cell(s).

Voila! As you look at the formula(s) in the pasted cell(s), you will see that it has changed relative to the row or column in which it resides. That is what *copying is relative* means.

Let's take a few moments to practice. Don't forget, sample data is available on my web site *www.lorrainestephens.com.*

Example – Copying formulas

Copy the formula that calculates the average for Rooks to calculate the individual averages for Givan, Stephens, Warrior and Carter.
1. Click in cell E2
2. Rest on the **Fill Handle**. Hold the mouse button down and drag the fill handle to E6.
3. Look at the formulas in E3 through E6. They have changed relative to the row in which they now reside.

	E
1	Average
2	=AVERAGE(B2:C2)
3	=AVERAGE(B3:C3)
4	=AVERAGE(B4:C4)
5	=AVERAGE(B5:C5)
6	=AVERAGE(B6:C6)

Example – Copying formulas

Calculate the total points scored in Game 2 by copying the formula from total points scored in Game 1.

1. Select **B7**.
2. Rest your mouse pointer on the **Fill Handle**. Hold down the mouse button and drag the **Fill Handle** to cell C7.
3. Release the mouse button.

	B	C
1	Score – Game 1	Score- Game 2
2	13	21
3	20	18
4	15	17
5	18	19
6	10	18
7	=SUM(B2:B6)	=SUM(C2:C6)

When you highlight a range of cells, the first cell does not look selected. Don't worry - it is. That is typical of the "active" cell.

Active Cell – the cell where data would appear if you started typing.

While you're on a roll, let's try another example.

Example – AutoSum and copying formulas

Use the AutoSum feature to add up the total that Rooks scored for the two games. Copy the formula to calculate the points scored by the other players for the two games.

1. Click in cell D2.
2. Double-click **AutoSum** to add up the scores for Rooks .
3. Click in cell D2.
4. Drag the fill handle down to D6

Notice how the formulas have adjusted relative to the rows.

	A	B	C	D
1	Name	Score – Game 1	Score- Game 2	Total
2	Rooks	13	21	=SUM(B2:C2)
3	Givan	20	18	=SUM(B3:C3)
4	Stephens	15	17	=SUM(B4:C4)
5	Warrior	18	19	=SUM(B5:C5)
6	Carter	10	18	=SUM(B6:C6)
7	Total Scored	=SUM(B2:B6)		

Good news! We are finished using this worksheet. The following examples will use different sets of data.

Relative vs. Absolute Cell Copying

When formulas with relative cell references are copied, its cell reference changes to adjust to the new location. Absolute cell references don't change when the formula is copied. An absolute reference is indicated by a dollar sign ($) in front of the column letter and row number (A1).

You create an absolute reference by pressing the **F4** key or by typing a $ in front of the row and column letter.
1. Click in the cell where the formula is to appear.
2. Type the formula.
3. Position the insertion point before the cell reference that you wish to make absolute.
4. Change it to an absolute formula by pressing **F4**.
5. Continue to press **F4** until the formula has a $ in front of the row number, and in front of the column letter.
6. Press **Enter**.

Let's put your learning to good use by calculating the score increase.

Example – Calculate the score increase

How many additional points per game will each player score if he increases his score by 15%? Use the worksheet below.

- ◆ The current scores are in cells D4:D8.
- ◆ The number representing the planned % increase is in C1.
- ◆ The planned increase amount for Rooks goes in G4.
- ◆ That formula is then to be copied down through G8.

1. Click in cell G4.
2. Type **=D4*C1**.
3. Position your cursor in the formula bar in front of the C1 entry.
4. Press the **F4** key on your keyboard until the C1 entry is C1.
5. Press the **Enter** key.
6. Copy the formula from G4 down through G8.

	A	B	C	D	E	F	G
1	Planned % increase		15%				
2							
3	Name	Score – Game 1	Score-Game 2	Total Score	Average		Planned Score Increase
4	Rooks	13	21	34	17		=D4*C1
5	Givan	20	18	38	19		=D5*C1
6	Stephens	15	17	32	16		=D6*C1
7	Warrior	18	19	37	18.5		=D7*C1
8	Carter	10		10	10		=D8*C1

Notice the formulas. The reference to cell C1 never changed. If we would not have made it an **absolute reference**, C1 would have changed to C2, C3, C4, and C5 as it was copied down. That would have caused errors in the formulas, and an error in formulas can cause indigestion. Now let's prepare to move a formula. If this is beginning to sound good to you – you are hooked!

MOVE A FORMULA

When you move a formula it does not change the formula like copying does.

1. Highlight and right-click the cell(s) that contains the formula you wish to move.
2. Select **Cut**.
3. Right-click the cell where you want to move the formula.
4. Select **Paste**.

Notice that the formula has not changed even though it is in a new location.

CREATING 3-D FORMULAS

3-D formulas perform calculations combining cell contents from different worksheets.

Example

Use 3-D formulas to calculate the income for the first quarter. The first quarter income is the sum of the income from January, February, and March. Refer to the worksheets that follow.

Notice that the formula for *1st Quarter Sales* is a different format than the formula for *1st Quarter Research*. One uses

operators, the other uses a **function**. Using a function decreases the amount that has to be typed or selected. Both methods are listed below. You choose the one that you prefer.

	A	B
1	January	
2		
3	Department	Income
4	Sales	450,000
5	Research	800,000
6	Marketing	300,000

	A	B
1	February	
2		
3	Department	Income
4	Sales	200,000
5	Research	700,000
6	Marketing	600,000

	A	B
1	March	
2		
3	Department	Income
4	Sales	9,000
5	Research	851,000
6	Marketing	510,000

	A	B
1		1st Quarter
2		
3	Department	Income
4	Sales	=January!B4+February!B4+March!B4
5	Research	=SUM(January:March!B5)
6	Marketing	=SUM(January:March!B6)

Method I
(Shown in cell B4 of the 1st Quarter sheet)
1. Click in cell B4 of the 1st Quarter worksheet.
2. Type =
3. Click the tab for the **January** worksheet.
4. Click cell B4.
5. Type +
6. Click the tab for the **February** worksheet.
7. Click in B4.
8. Type +
9. Click the tab for the **March** worksheet.
10. Click in B4.
11. Press the **Enter** key.

Method II
(Shown in cells B5 and B6 of the 1st Quarter sheet)
1. Click in cell B5 of the 1st Quarter worksheet.
2. Type =SUM(
3. Click the tab for the **January** worksheet.
4. Click cell B5.
5. If the February and March worksheets follow the January worksheet hold down the **Shift** key and click the **March** worksheet tab.
6. If the **February** and **March** worksheets do not follow the January worksheet but are mixed in with other sheets, hold down the **Ctrl** key and click the February worksheet tab and the March worksheet tab.
7. Press the **Enter** key.

81

Whichever method you use to calculate the 3D formula is fine.

> The second one will save you a lot of keystrokes and cell selection. However it only works if the cell reference is in the same place on each worksheet.

NOT REALLY FORMULAS – JUST "GOLDEN NUGGETS"

These were just too good to omit, but they did not fall under the title of formulas. So let's just call these "Golden Nuggets."

AutoCalculate

When you want to quickly find the sum, average, maximum, minimum, or count figures use this feature of Excel.

1. Highlight the cells you want to calculate.
2. Look in the status bar of your worksheet and you will see a value. (It might say Sum= or Average=….). That is your AutoCalculate feature.
3. Right-click on the AutoCalculate feature and select the function that you want.
   It's as simple as that.

Conditional Formatting

When you are formatting the cells that will contain data, you may wish to highlight data that meets certain conditions. For example you decide that any item that has a unit cost greater than $8000 should print as bold and dark red. Conditional formatting will accomplish this for you. Conditional Formatting will allow you to set up to three

conditions for the cell(s) being tested. Let's take a look at the procedure.

1. Select the cell(s) that you wish to format based on value.
2. Select **Format>Conditional Formatting**.
3. Choose the condition and the formatting for the first condition.
4. Select **Add** to add a second condition.
5. Choose the condition and the formatting for the second condition.

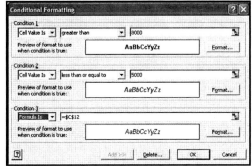

6. Select **Add** to add a third condition.
7. Choose the condition and the formatting for the third condition.
8. Select **OK** when finished.

Pretty simple and straightforward, isn't it? Once the criteria is set, any data entered into the conditionally formatted cell will be tested and formatted according to your settings.

Fill series

A quick method to enter data into a worksheet is to use the **Fill Series** statement. The four types are shown in the **Series** dialog box. A series can be across a row or down a column.

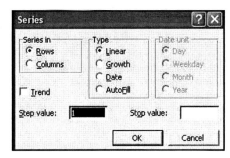

An example of a **Linear** series is:

1, 2, 3, 4, 5 or 3, 6, 9, 12. The difference between these two linear series is the **Step Value**. The first one has a step value of 1. The second one has a step value of 3.

An example of a **Growth** series is:

2, 4, 8, 16, 32. This one starts with 2 and has a step value of 2. This growth series is calculated by multiplying 2*2*2*2. The **Stop Value** tells the series what number indicates the end of the series.

The **Date** series gives you the options of everyday, weekday, month or year. For example, a date of 3/1/2006 showing weekdays and stopping at 3/9/2006 would result in:

3/1/2006	3/2/2006	3/3/2006	3/6/2006	3/7/2006	3/8/2006	3/9/2006

Notice that the weekends are missing. (I guess we could say that this feature takes the weekends off.)

The **AutoFill** is one of the greatest tools for setting up a schedule or similar worksheets. This helpful feature allows you to list times, dates, names, etc. If you type 9:00 into a cell and use the AutoFill feature it will list 10:00, 11:00, 12:00, etc. Here are a few quick examples.

AutoFill Examples

Creating a listing of times starting at 9:00
1. Type **9:00** in cell A1.
2. Press the **Enter** key.
3. Highlight A1 through A10.
4. Select **Edit>Fill>Series>AutoFill>OK**.
5. The default will show a series of:

9:00 10:00 11:00 12:00 13:00 14:00 15:00 16:00 17:00 18:00

Create a listing of times 45 minutes apart and starting at 9:00
1. Type **9:00** in cell A1.
2. Type **9:45** in cell A2.
3. Highlight A1 through A10.
4. Select **Edit>Fill>Series>AutoFill>OK**.

Automatically Listing names
This is a two part procedure. The first part is to create a custom list. The second part is to use the custom list in a series.
1. Create the custom list if it is not already created.
   a Type your list of names into the spreadsheet – one name in each cell.
   b Highlight the list of names.
   c Select **Tools>Options>Custom List** tab**>Import>OK**.
2. Use the custom list in your series.
   a Click in a blank cell.
   b Type the first name in the list.
   c Position your cursor on the **AutoFill** handle.
   d Drag the fill handle down or across.

This will automatically fill the rows or columns with the names in your list.

Congratulations! You've completed this section on formulas. Did you pick up any useful tips? I hope so. As you burrow deeper into Excel you will find more "golden nuggets". You're probably thinking; "If I had only known all of this stuff yesterday, it would have made my life much easier." The important thing is you know it now. Here is a special toast to you and your progress.

Keyboard Shortcuts

There are numerous keyboard shortcuts. Here are some of the ones that I personally find most useful. A full list can be found in the Excel help screens.

Description	Shortcut
Add a second line in a cell	Alt + Enter
Apply the comma format with two decimal places	Ctrl + Shift + !
Convert a calculated value into a fixed value (This will delete the formula but keep the calculated value of the field)	• Click in the cell • Click in the formula bar • Press F9
Convert time from 24 hour military time to AM or PM	Ctrl + Shift+@
Copy	Ctrl + C
Create a chart/graph	• Highlight the data • Press F11
Cut	Ctrl + X
Display range names	F3
Format Bold	Ctrl + B
Format Italics	Ctrl + I
Format Underline	Ctrl + U
Go to previous sheet	Ctrl+ PgUp
Go to the first row	Ctrl + up arrow
Go to the last row	Ctrl + down arrow
Go to the next worksheet	Ctrl+ PgDn
Insert a new worksheet	Shift + F11
Insert current date	Ctrl + ;
Insert current time	Ctrl + Shift + ;
Move to the beginning of the row	Home
Move to the beginning of the worksheet	Ctrl+ Home
Move to the end of the worksheet	Ctrl+ End
Open the format cell dialog box	Ctrl+1
Paste	Ctrl + V
Repeat the entry that is in the cell above	Ctrl + "

Description	Shortcut
Repeat the last action (Whatever action you performed last, do it again)	Ctrl + Y
Select a column	Ctrl + Space Bar
Select a range of cells	1. Click the first cell 2. Hold the Shift key 3. Click the last cell
Select a row	Shift + Space Bar
Select all cells that contain comments	Ctrl + Shift + O
Select the entire worksheet	Ctrl+ A
Show/Hide formulas	Ctrl + ~

 Do not type the plus symbol. It is used here to indicate more than one key is being held down at the same time.

" " Computers are magnificent tools for the realization of our dreams, but no machine can replace the human spark of spirit, compassion, love, and understanding. " "

Louis Gerstner

Creating Charts & Graphs

*L*earning how to use charts to display data can be the start of a wonderful experience. Look at the data shown. Which one immediately tells a story? Is it the one with the numeric data? Or, is it the chart with pictures and columns? Most will agree that the chart tells the story right away. Why? Because a picture is worth a thousand words.

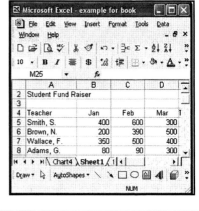

Immediately you can see where your top performers are; amounts were low in January;

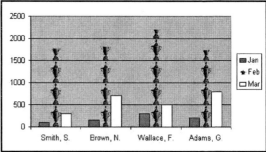

and exceptionally high in February. It is for this reason

that charts are an excellent method of presenting information. They show graphical relationships of information.

Each value in a chart is called a **Data Point**. The columns and the rows are called **Data Series**. For example, there is a January data series in the worksheet. There is also a Smith data series, along with several others. What if I told you that you could create a chart in less time than it takes you to read this sentence? You really can. Here's how.

CREATING A CHART
(IN JUST SIX SECONDS!)

Creating a chart is almost too simple. In fact you can create one in just six seconds. Be sure to include the row and column headings in your highlighted cells since the chart uses for labels.

Get ready and time yourself – six seconds maximum and you will have a chart!
1. Click in the first cell that is to be a part of the chart. (Do not forget your labels.)
2. Hold down the **Shift** key.
3. Click in the last cell that is to be a part of the chart. (Your data and headings should now be highlighted.)
4. Release the **Shift** key.
5. Press the **F11** key.

Voila. It is almost too simple.

EDITING YOUR CHART

Once the chart is created, you can change any and all parts of it to look the way you want.

There are four commands under the **Chart** menu item that assist with all chart editing. The commands are:

◆ Chart Type
◆ Source Data
◆ Chart Options
◆ Location

Choosing a chart type

Chart type — The Chart type option allows you to change the chart to the type that you desire. There are many to choose from (bar, column, pie, line, scatter, area, radar and many others).

What is very important is that you choose the chart type that clearly demonstrates the story you wish to tell. For example, a pie chart would not be a good chart to display the data in this worksheet. A bar, line or column might be better. Why? Because a pie chart could only

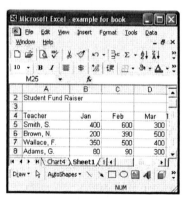

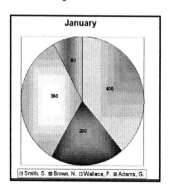

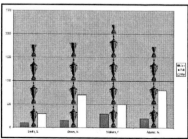

show the information for *one* of the three months, or for *one* of the four people.

1. While on the chart sheet, select **Chart>Chart Type**.
2. Select the **Standard types** tab.
3. Select the **Chart type** on the left, and the **Chart sub-type** on the right.
4. Select **OK**.

 If you do not see a chart type you wish to use under the Standard tab, select the Custom tab and see your choices there.

 Don't forget the almighty right-click. Just in case you have not discovered it, clicking the right mouse button (commonly referred to as "right-clicking") will give you many of the same options as double-clicking or using the menu bar. Try it while pointing to a part of your chart.

Changing the source data

This simply means changing the data you used for your chart.

Source Data – The source data option allows you to add columns and/or rows to your data range. The option is on the **Data Range** tab of the **Source Data** dialog box.

 Data range – the selected information (data) being included in your graph.

You are also able to switch between showing the data in columns, or showing it in rows. This option is noted on the **Series** tab. As you study the graphs below, notice how they

both show the same data. However, one of them is grouping the data by each month. The other is grouping the data by each person. The first one would be a good way to demonstrate the high performance month for each person. The second one would be a good way to demonstrate the high performance person for each month.

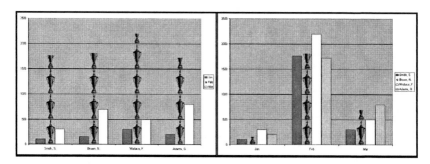

The **Series** tab of the Source Data dialog box gives you the ability to add or remove information. For example, if you did not want to show February in the chart, simply select the February series from the series listing and click **Remove**.

1. Select **Chart>Source Data**.
2. Select **Data Range** tab.
3. Verify or change the data range that is shown.

   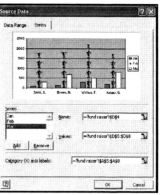

   a. You may change it by clicking the red arrow to collapse the window.
   b. Notice the marquee going around the data that is currently a part of the graph.
   c. If this is correct, select the red dot again to expand the dialog box. If it is not, highlight the data you want to graph.
4. Select whether you want your chart to be in row series or in column series. Notice the difference in

your graph as you switch between row and column. The preview is very helpful.

5. Select the **Series** tab.

6. If you want to delete any of the series listed, select it and click the **Remove** button.

7. To add a series :
   a. Select **Add**.
   b. Click in the **Name** text box - this is where you will tell the system to look for the name of the series you are adding.
   c. Collapse the dialog box by selecting the **red arrow** in the Name box.
   d. Highlight the cell in your spreadsheet that has the name of the other row or column you are adding – *just the name.* (You may have to select the tab of your worksheet in order to see your data.)
   e. Select the **red dot** again to expand the dialog box. The name box is now added. The only thing missing is telling the system where to find the values for that named field.
   f. Click in the **Values** text box – this is where you will tell the system where to find the values for the series you are adding.
   g. Click the **red arrow** to collapse the dialog box.
   h. Select the cells that contain the values for the added series.
   i. Expand the dialog box by clicking the red dot.
   j. Select **OK**.

The values you add do not have to be from the same worksheet or from the same workbook. This is a great tool if you are creating a chart to compare data shown in different workbooks.

Any questions? Remember "source data" simply means the information (or data) you are using for your chart.

Selecting the chart options

Chart options allow you to add titles to your chart, determine what axes will show, decide how many gridlines to have, decide if you will have a legend and where the legend should be, decide if your data points should show their value, decide if the data in the spreadsheet should be shown beneath your chart, and much more. I realize that was a mouth full so you may want to read that sentence again. Let's see how it works.

1. Select **Chart>Chart Options**.
2. Select the various tabs, take a look at them, and choose your options.
3. Select **OK**.

As you go through the tabs most of them will be self-explanatory. However, there are a few points to consider that I would like to list for you.

1. **Titles** tab
   a. The more titles you enter, the smaller the area for your graph.
2. **Axis** tab
   a. Not showing an axis that contains your values is all right if that meets your needs.
   b. If you decide to eliminate the axis with the values and still want to show the values, you may do so by selecting the **Data Labels** tab and selecting to show the data **Value**.
3. **Legend** tab – The legend is a small box that explains what each color means.

a. Placing your legend on the top or bottom of your chart allows more room for you chart to spread out horizontally.

b. If you are going to show the data table on the chart and include the legend there, you can choose not to check **Show Legend** on this tab.

c. Even though you can move the legend manually by selecting it and dragging it to a new location, I recommend you allow Excel to do this for you through the **Legend** tab. When Excel moves it for you, it will adjust the chart. When you move it yourself, the chart size and location will not automatically adjust. Let the software save you time and energy.

4. **Data Labels** tab

a. Though good to use on some charts, it might appear cluttered on others. Pie charts lend themselves well to data labels. If you are not charting a large number of columns or bars, data labels can add to the meaning of your chart. If using line charts, they can be especially helpful.

It might be helpful to talk about where your chart is going to appear. That is referred to as "chart location."

Choosing the chart location

There are only three places your chart can be:

1. Sharing a sheet with your data;

2. Sharing a sheet with another chart;

3. On a sheet by itself.

This option allows you to

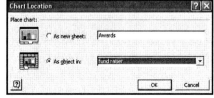

move your chart to one of these locations.

1. Select **Chart>Location**. (If the chart is on the same page as your data, you must select the chart before you begin this step.)
2. If it is going to be on its own sheet:
   a. Click **As new sheet**.
   b. Name the chart sheet.
3. If it is going to share a sheet with data or another chart.
   a. Click **As object in**.
   b. Select the name of the sheet or chart from the drop-down arrow.
4. Select **OK**.

FORMATTING CHARTS

Formatting charts consist of changing the colors, shapes, appearance of data points, etc. Since each part of a chart can be formatted, you can become very creative. You will notice that the February data series on this chart is formatted with clip art. Everything from the gray background (plot area) to the fonts used can be changed to suit your preference. Here's how you do it.

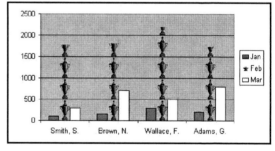

1. Point to the area you wish to format. As you point to the area a tool-tip will pop up verifying the area selected.
2. Double-click on the area.
3. Choose from the formatting options given.

 One word of caution. Charts are very sensitive. Be sure you are pointing to exactly what you want to format when you double-click. Otherwise you will not open the dialog box that you are expecting to open.

If you double-click the axis of the chart you will see that you can change everything about the axis.

Patterns tab:

♦ Appearance of the line

♦ Placement of labels – **Tick Mark Labels** is Excel-ese for the labels on your axis that identify your information. In our chart, the labels are Smith, Brown, Wallace and Adams. If you wanted those at the top of your chart rather than the bottom, you would choose "high" under the section **Tick Mark Labels**.

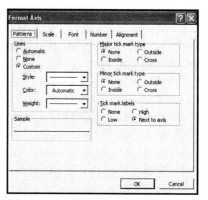

Scale tab:

♦ Have the axis switch from the left side to the right, or the top to the bottom - Choose Values in Reverse Order.

Font tab:

♦ Determine the font type, style, size, color, etc.

Number tab:

♦ Format numbers for date, currency, percentage, etc.

Alignment tab:

♦ Change the direction of your text.

If you double-click on the **Plot Area,** you have the option of changing the color and pattern.

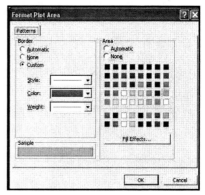

If you double-click on the line of a line graph, you can change the width, color, data point markers, and so much more.

If you double-click a section of a pie chart or bar chart, you can change the color, shape, etc.

If you double-click the gridlines, you will have the option of changing the appearance of the lines. There are two tabs.

1. Patterns – Controls the pattern of the line (weight, color, etc.).
2. Scale – Changes the high and the low numbers on the plotting scale, and the number meanings of the gridlines.

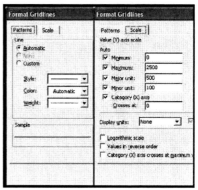

Feel free to double-click on each part of the chart and format it to suit your fancy.

This is a very helpful feature. Don't you agree? You might even want to include pictures to represent your data. This is a favorite for me.

Using pictures to represent data

In the previous chart you will notice that one data series is represented by a trophy. You can use any picture you desire. If you are presenting financial data, using something repre-

senting currency may enhance your graph. The idea is to tell your story in the best and clearest manner possible.

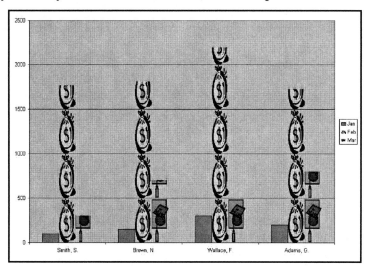

This graph uses graduation caps for one of the data series. This would be a great way to demonstrate the number of students that graduated. Setting each one to represent five hundred students quickly shows how our range goes from two-hundred fifty to a little over seven-hundred fifty students.

It also uses moneybags to represent a different data series. If you indicate to your audience that each of the moneybags represents five hundred dollars it is quickly visible how much money each data series represents. The procedure for using pictures to represent data is elementary my dear reader. Here's how it works.

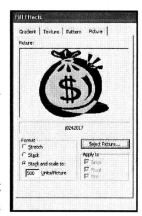

1. Double-click the bar on the chart representing the data series you wish to format with a picture.

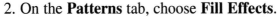

2. On the **Patterns** tab, choose **Fill Effects**.

3. Choose the **Picture** tab.

4. Choose the **Select Picture** button.

5. Select the drive and folder where your desired picture is found.

6. Select the picture that you wish to use. (Often you will want to use clip art. So, look in the folder where your clip art is stored.)

7. Choose **Insert**.

8. It is now time to decide how your moneybags are going to look.

   a. Will you stretch one moneybag to represent the amount on your graph?

   b. Will you stack the moneybags?

   c. If you are going to stack the moneybags, how much will each moneybag represent?

   Make the selection under the **Format** section of the **Picture** tab.

9. Select **OK**.

10. Select **OK**.

 You may use gradients, patterns, and textures for formatting chart object. Follow the same steps as outlined in steps 1 and 2. Then select the pattern, texture, or gradient tab to determine your fill pattern. Be creative. Have fun.

Have you noticed there is a certain Donald Trump charm that comes with playing with money, even it it's only clipart money? The important thing is you've learned how to use pictures to represent data. We are ready to move on to printing your chart.

PRINTING YOUR CHART

1. If your chart is on it's own sheet, click the sheet tab that contains your chart. Select **File>Print>OK**.
2. If your chart is on the same sheet as your data, click the sheet tab that contains your data. Click your chart. Select **File>Print>OK**.

USING THE CHART TOOLBAR

By now, you have discovered a toolbar that appears when you are working on a chart. It is called the **Chart Toolbar**. This is about as descriptive as you can get – it tells you what type of toolbar we're dealing with. Many of the options listed in the menu bar under **Chart** are included in the Chart Toolbar.

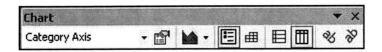

You've got plenty of options to work with because there are nine buttons on this toolbar. Reading from left to right, their functions are:

1. Select an area of the chart to format.
2. Format the selected area.
3. Change the chart type.
4. Show or hide the legend.
5. Show or hide the data-table.
6. Display data by row.
7. Display data by column.
8. Angle the selected text down. [Text must be selected before this will work]
9. Angle the selected text up. [Text must be selected before this will work]

Summary

If you are planning to create charts from your data, keep that very important fact in mind as you determine how to layout your data on your worksheet. For example if you wanted to chart data for three clients by time, by activity, which one of the layout methods below would you use for entering your data? The one used in rows 1 through 4? Or the one used in rows 6 through 9?

	A	B	C	D	E	F	G	H	I	J	K	L	M	N	O	P
1		ABC, Inc.	Jan 1-15	Jan 16-31	Feb 1-15	Feb 15-29	FUN, Inc.	Jan 1-15	Jan 16-31	Feb 1-15	Feb 15-29	LSA, Inc	Jan 1-15	Jan 16-31	Feb 1-15	Feb 15
2	Contacts made		3	4	6	4		3	8	6	4		3	0	6	
3	Sales calls		4	2	5	2		4	2	7	2		4	9	7	
4	Executive visits		5	3	1	4		4	2	1	6		1	2	6	
5																
6	Activity	ABC, Inc. Jan 1-15	ABC, Inc. Jan 16-31	ABC, Inc. Feb 1-15	ABC, Inc. Feb 15-29	FUN, Inc. Jan 1-15	FUN, Inc. Jan 16-31	FUN, Inc. Feb 1-15	FUN, Inc. Feb 15-29	LSA, Inc Jan 1-15	LSA, Inc Jan 16-31	LSA, Inc Feb 1-15	LSA, Inc Feb 15-29			
7	Contacts made	3	4	6	4	3	8	6	4	3	0	6	4			
8	Sales calls	4	2	5	2	4	2	7	2	4	9	7	3			
9	Executive visits	5	3	1	4	4	2	1	6	1	2	6	6			

I would recommend the data as entered in rows 6 through 9. Why?

1. All of the labels needed in your graph are together – It is going to be difficult to graph the figures for all three companies in one graph using the data entry method displayed in rows 1 through 4.

2. Charting "Contacts made", or "Sales calls", or "Executive visits" individually is easy since you have supplied an appropriate header for this field in A6. The first example does not have a field header in cell A1.

When formatting your chart it does not matter if you double-click, use the toolbar, or right-click. What does matter is your becoming comfortable with the knowledge that you are in control of the way it will look. So go for it! Chart and format to your heart's content.

Designing Your Excel Worksheet

*I*n Chapter One, there is a section on *Setting Up A Basic Worksheet.* You may want to review this section for some design considerations. In this chapter we will build on those elements and include such topics as:

- Additional layout considerations
- Inserting comments
- Merging of cells
- Determining what calculations are required

- Validating that the correct data is being entered
- Conditional formatting
- Inserting desired graphics
- Automatically filling columns

LAYOUT CONSIDERATIONS

As you read through this detailed list of layout considerations please refer to the worksheet following the list. Take your time and digest these layout considerations. There is a lot of information in this small area.

Part 1	
Enter column headings	When I design a worksheet, my initial focus is always the column headers needed to identify my data lists. Normally this requires my starting in the middle of my worksheet and working my way down then up. Once my data area is designed, I know how much space I have for the rest of my worksheet, and what size or location limitations are placed on my headings.
Size the columns	Based on the size of the data that will be entered you will want to adjust your column width. Do not base your column width on the size of your column heading. You can wrap the text in the column headings to enable the text to fit into the cell.
Format cells	Bold, currency, number of decimal places, fill color etc. For a little different look, try using a dark fill color and white or light colored text for your headings.
Align cells	By default, numeric data will be right aligned while alphanumeric data will be left aligned. If you wish to change the alignment of data when it is typed into the cell, highlight those cells and chose what their alignment should be. Consider formatting cells to enable text wrapping. This will allow for cell content longer than the column is wide.

Part 1, continued

Enter formulas	Enter the formulas needed. The formulas needed in the example shown are: ◆ Total price (placed in F11) ◆ Subtotal (placed in F40) ◆ Tax (placed in F41) ◆ Total (placed in F43) ◆ Calculate Payment Due (placed in F8) [in this worksheet the formula in F8 is: =F43] Remember you can copy formulas down once they are entered.
Copy formulas	Copy your formulas down or across as needed. Once you determine which formulas to copy, it will eliminate the need to type the formula in every row. In this example, the formula is placed in F11 and copied from F11 to F38.
Put borders around data	If desired, place borders around your data. This is optional and is more significant for printing than for data entry.
Determine page orientation	If your worksheet is wide, you might want to make it a landscape page.
Adjust margins if necessary	If your worksheet is just a little too wide, adjust the margins on the right and the left to make them narrower.

Part 2	
Put in identifying information	You're now ready to enter the company name, address, titles, graphics, etc.
Merge cells where necessary	Chances are you will need to merge some of the cells. In this example, "Invoice" is entered in cell A1. In order for it to be centered across the page we used the **Merge and Center** feature. "Invoice number" and Invoice date" are also merged and centered.
Format graphics	If you have added graphics to your worksheet, enhancing the graphics with color, shading, or 3D style will enhance your worksheet.
Shade cells	Consider adding shading or patterns to some of your cells. This will enhance the appearance of the worksheet and help the user know where info is to be found or entered.

MERGE CELLS

When you need a cell to be wider or taller but you do not wish to increase the row height or the column width, merging cells is a feature you may wish to use. We will examine two methods:
- ◆ Using the right-click
- ◆ Using the merge cells icon

	A	B	C	D	E	F	G
1			Invoice				
2							
3	L. . Stephens & Associates, Inc.				Invoice date		
4	The Education & Technology Group				Invoice number		
5	www.lorrainestephens.com						
6	(919) 876-3100	Quality Service					
7		& Support		2			
8					Payment due		
9							
10	Date	Item Number	Description	Qty	Unit Price	Total Price	
11						$ -	
12						$ -	
13						$ -	
14						$ -	
15						$ -	
16						$ -	
17						$ -	
18						$ -	
19						$ -	
20						$ -	
21						$ -	
22						$ -	
23						$ -	
24						$ -	
25						$ -	
26						$ -	
27						$ -	
28						$ -	
29						$ -	
30						$ -	
31						$ -	
32						$ -	
33						$ -	
34						$ -	
35						$ -	
36						$ -	
37						$ -	
38						$ -	
39						$ -	
40					Subtotal	$ -	
41					Tax	$ -	
42					Shipping		
43					Total	$ -	

To merge two or more cells into one cell:
1. Highlight the cells.
2. Right-click in the highlighted area.
3. Select **Format Cells**.
4. Select the **Alignment** tab.
5. Select **Merge Cells**.

You can also add the **Merge Cells** icon to your toolbar if it is not there. This is found in the chapter **Customizing Toolbars**.

To use the toolbar icon to merge cells:
1. Highlight the cells to be merged.
2. Click the **Merge Cells** icon.

MERGE CELLS ACROSS

The Merge Cells feature will take all of the highlighted cells and merge them into one cell. However, this is not always what you want to occur. For example if you wanted cells B2:B4 to merge into one cell, **Merge Cells** would work fine. However, if you wanted the same merging to happen across C2:C4, and D2:D4, and E2:E4, you would find that highlighting them all then choosing Merge Cells would merge all of your cells into one cell. **Merge Cells Across** is the feature you would want to use for this task. It will merge your highlighted row cells into one cell on each row.

Since finding this little "hidden" feature, I have saved myself hours of time. It is no longer necessary to merge cells one row at a time.

1. Add the **Merge Across** icon to your toolbar. (It is found under the **Format** command.)

2. Highlight the cells in the rows that you wish to merge.
3. Click **Merge Across**.

Now would be a good time, I suppose, to mention how to quickly fill in rows and columns.

FILLING ROWS AND COLUMNS

Excel offers the ability to fill rows and columns automatically with a feature called **Fill Series**. Some of the data that you enter will trigger to Excel that an automatic fill feature is available, while others will require special handling.

For example, if you type any of the following into a cell, you can automatically fill the row or column.

If you type:	Automatic fill will give you:
1st Quarter	2nd Quarter, 3rd Quarter, 4th Quarter
1st period	2nd period, 3rd period, 4th period…..
Monday	Tuesday, Wednesday ……
January	February, March, April….
March 1, 2004	March 2, 2004, March 3, 2004…….
8:00	9:00, 10:00, 11:00……..(You may need to format the time once you use the fill handle to complete it. Normally it will use military time)

1. Type your entry into the cell.
2. Rest your mouse pointer on the fill handle. (The fill handle is a small box located in the lower right hand corner of the cell. When your pointer is placed on it, the pointer will become a small black cross hair.)
3. Hold the mouse button down and drag up or down to fill a column; or right or left to fill the row.
4. If you drag the fill handle up or left notice that it places the data in the cells in the reverse order.
5. Release the mouse button when finished.

There are far more automatic fill sequences than we will cover. Feel free to experiment. Having access to this quick way of setting up your row or column headings will save you a great deal of time. The chapter *No More Mysteries About Formulas,* has additional information on using the fill feature.

If you've got the time and the inclination, let's see how to prepare your worksheet for entering data.

PREPARING FOR DATA ENTRY

Validating data

Once your worksheet is setup to accept your data, you may wish to test the validity of some of the data. You can establish the minimum and maximum values allowed for a cell, allow only dates, or allow only whole numbers. For example, if shipping cost must be $4.25 or more, you can force data validation to test the amount typed into the shipping cost field and to give an error message if it is invalid.

When you select a cell that is using data validation, a tip will appear letting you know that the cell will accept only a certain type of data. When invalid data is entered into the cell a message will inform you the data is invalid. Depending on how you have designed your data validation, other people who use your worksheet will have a choice of ignoring the rule and continuing with the invalid data, or changing the data to fit within the description of what is valid.

- Enabling data validation -

1. Select the cells where you want to check the data that is entered.
2. From the menu bar select **Data>Validation**.
3. Select the **Settings** tab. Set your criteria based on:

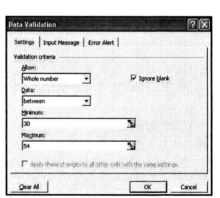

a. What you will **Allow**
b. What the **Data** comparison is
c. Your **Minimum**, your **Maximum**, or your **Value** for comparison. This section will change based on the

choice you make in the **Data** text box. The value entered can be a constant or can reference a cell on you worksheet.

4. Select the **Input Message** tab. Type in your title and message. (Your message will appear in a tip window when this cell is selected. The message has a title and a message area. In this example the title is "Whole numbers only". The message is "Value must be between 30 and 54".)

> **Whole numbers only**
> Value must be between 30 and 54

5. Select the **Error Alert** tab. Here you indicate what should happen when invalid data is typed in. There are three options you may choose from for handling invalid data.

Style:
Stop

a. **Stop** – this does not allow the user to enter that value into the cell.

b. **Warning** – the user receives a message indicating this value is outside of the range of valid entries. It will, however, allow the entry to be made into the cell once the user acknowledges it as being acceptable.

Style:
Warning

c. **Information** - the user receives a warning indicating this entry is outside of a valid range of entries. It will, however, allow the entry into the cell

Style:
Information

Type in the title and the message that should appear when invalid data is entered into the cell. An example of a **Warning** message dialog box is seen here.

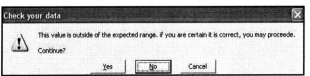

Check your data

This value is outside of the expected range. if you are certain it is correct, you may proceede.
Continue?

Yes   No   Cancel

Once you have set the cells for data validation, locked the cells, and protected the worksheet, no one can change this without the password. (See the chapter on *Creating Templates* for locking cells and protecting worksheets.) Don't forget the password! If so, even you cannot change it. (I am sure someone is already saying they can hack into it and change it, or purchase a special utility to change it – and they are right. However, for you, the average person – *please don't forget your password!*)

- Highlight data based on values-
Conditional Formatting -

When you are formatting cells which will contain data, you may wish to highlight data based on certain conditions. For example, you desire any item with a unit greater than $8000 to print as bold and dark red. Conditional formatting will accomplish this for you. Conditional Formatting will allow you to set up to three conditions for the cell(s) being tested. Once the criteria are set, any data entered into the conditionally formatted cell will be tested and formatted according to your settings.

See the chapter *No More Mysteries About Formulas* for this procedure.

Now, let's move on to comments. Whenever you prepare documents in any application, it is recommended to include some type of documentation. In Excel, comments can serve as a form of documentation. I think you will like this feature.

ADDING COMMENTS TO YOUR WORKSHEET

Comments – Sticky notes

Normally comments are entered to look like yellow sticky notes.

1. Right-click in the cell where the comment will appear.
2. Select **Insert Comment**.
3. Type the comment.
4. Press the **Enter** key.
5. A small red triangle will appear in the corner of the cell with the comment.
6. To see the comments rest on the red triangle.
7. To view all of the comments select **View Comments**.
8. To print the comments:
   a. Select **File>Page Setup**.
   b. Click the Sheet tab.
   c. Next to the **Comments** area select **As displayed on sheet** or **At end of sheet**.

That's all there is to it. But let's take a peek at another way of entering comments.

Comments- in the formula bar

Another way of entering comments is to place them directly in the cell with the formula. This method is useful as a method of documentation by the person designing the worksheet. This comment will be very much appreciated when you have moved on to a new position and someone else needs to modify your worksheet.

1. Enter your formula in the desired cell
2. Enter your comment after the formula using this format:

N("this is my comment")

Therefore, an example of your cell content showing the formula and the comment could be:

=Average(A1:B5) +N("This information came from the annual report")

3. The cell will show the answer resulting from averaging A1 through B5.
4. When you click in the cell the comment will show in the formula bar along with the rest of the formula.

That's all there is to entering comments as a part of the formula content.

Now it is time for a little fun – a little light stuff. Let's get ready to insert graphics into the worksheet.

INSERTING GRAPHICS

Graphics can truly enhance the appearance of your worksheet. In fact I recommend them. They are a wonderful enhancement. For example, a picture of your building at the top makes an attractive worksheet. Excel versions after 2000, have included the capability to insert pictures into headers and footers. Great feature! Be aware, however, graphics will increase the size of your file.

Insert your logo
As long as you know where to find your logo you can insert it on your worksheet.

1. Select **Insert>Pictures>From File.**
2. Select the drive and open the folder where the logo picture resides.
3. Select your logo.
4. Select **Insert.**

Since the logo is an object, it can be sized and moved as desired.

Insert pictures

1. Select **Insert>Pictures>From File.**
2. Select the drive and open the folder where the picture resides.
3. Select your picture.
4. Select **Insert.**

Since the picture is an object, it can be sized and moved as desired.

Insert clip art

1. Select **Insert>Pictures>Clip Art.**
2. Select the **Clip Art** desired.

At the risk of repeating myself again, since the clip art is an object, it can be sized and moved as desired.

Insert drawn objects

Use the **Drawing** toolbar to insert ovals, rectangles, lines, etc. In addition, you have a variety of **AutoShapes** available. If you do not see the drawing toolbar, **right-click** on the **Menu bar,** then click on **Drawing.**

1. Select the shape or **AutoShape** you want to draw.
2. Your mouse pointer becomes a cross-hair as you move it around on your worksheet.

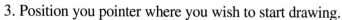

3. Position you pointer where you wish to start drawing.
4. Hold the mouse button down and draw your object. (Even if you are not a Michael Angelo, try drawing something.)
5. Apply a shadow with the shadow icon on the drawing toolbar. This gives your drawing a finished look.
6. Use the 3-D toolbar button to give the appearance of depth to the drawing.
7. Use the rotate tool to angle the drawing.

Once again, since the drawing is an object, it can be sized and moved as desired.

 You may wish to remember this little nugget of information, you cannot apply a shadow and a 3-D effect to the same graphic

Summary

Your layout will be as individualized as you are. Sociologist Joseph Campbell once said: "The privilege of life is to be who you are." So design your layouts to suit yourself. They have to meet your needs and be pleasing to your eye. I hope I have given you some items to consider.

Please become very familiar with formulas because formulas will be the key to enjoying and successfully using Excel as you are setting up your worksheet.

Creating and Using Templates

*W*ere it not for the wonderful invention of templates, we would spend a great deal of time reinventing the wheel. Templates afford us the ability of setting up a workbook with the desired formatting, graphics, formulas, and worksheets. Once done and saved as a template, you do not have to create the layout again.

CREATING A TEMPLATE

Creating a template consists of four easy steps. (Where have you heard that before?) Seriously though, if I go a bit overboard in my explanations it's because I want you to excel at Excel. The four steps outlined below are fundamental for creating templates.

   1. Format your worksheet. This means to decide where information is to be entered; what graphics you want to have; where the graphics will be; what shading and boarders you wish to use; what fonts you are going to use; how your numeric data and formulas will be formatted; etc.

2. Lock any cells you do not want to have changed. This prevents anyone from accidentally deleting formulas and other information. Unlock any cells where data will be typed when your template is being used.
3. Protect your worksheet.
4. Save your worksheet as a **Template**. This option is found in the **Save As Type** text box.

In order for you to create a template that will perform your desired calculations, I recommend that you familiarize yourself first with:

1. Creating formulas
2. Copying formulas
3. Formatting numbers and text
4. Formatting cells

Once you understand these areas, you will be able to focus on things needed to create an easy to use template.

Since earlier sections covered creating formulas and formatting information, I will start with the second step, unlocking cells.

LOCK/UNLOCK CELLS

All cells that will be used to type data into must be unlocked. By default, all cells are locked.

In the worksheet shown, the shaded

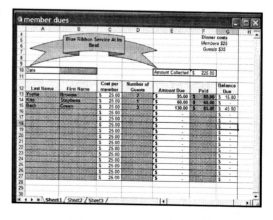

cells are the ones that will accept data; therefore they need to be unlocked.

- Date
- Last Name
- First Name
- Number of guests
- Paid

They must be available for the person using the template to enter data.

The other cells contain either formulas or constant information:

- Cost per member (constant)
- Amount Due (Formula - calculated based on the cost for the member and the number of guests attending)
- Balance due (Formula – the result of subtracting Paid from Amount Due)
- Amount Collected (Formula – the sum of Paid)

Since you do not want this information accidentally deleted, you want to leave them, along with your headings and graphics, locked.

Follow this procedure to unlock all cells where data will be entered by the user.

1. Highlight the cells that will accept data when your template is being used.
2. Select **Format>Cells>Protection** tab.
3. Remove the check mark from **Locked**.
4. Select **OK**.

The cells are now properly locked or unlocked. However, this will not take affect until you Protect the worksheet.

PROTECT WORKSHEET

1. From the menu bar select
   Tools>Protection>Protect Sheet. Your Protect
   Sheet dialog box will differ based on the version of
   Excel that you are using.

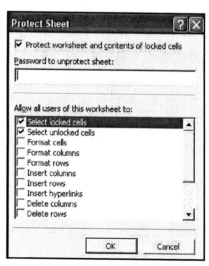

2. *For Office 2000:*
   a. Check all of the options
   b. Type a password.
   c. Press **OK**
   d. Retype the password
   e. Press **OK**

3. *For office XP:*
   a. Place a check mark
      in **Protect work-
      sheet and contents
      of locked cells**.
   b. Type your pass-
      word.
   c. You may place a
      check mark in any
      of the options
      listed under **Allow
      all users of this
      worksheet** if you
      want to allow users
      to make changes to
      your worksheet. Be careful with these options.
      Leave all of them unchecked until you are sure you
      want to give this freedom to your users.
   d. Press **OK**
   e. Retype the password.
   f. Press **OK**.

That's it. You're protected.

SAVE THE FILE AS A TEMPLATE

1. **File>Save As.**
2. In the File Name text box, type a name for your template.
3. In the save as type box select **Template.**
4. Select **Save.**

USE THE TEMPLATE

1. **File>New.**
2. Look on the **General** tab for your template. Template icons have a yellow stripe across the top and look like the one shown here. (In Office XP this will be in the Task Pane. In Office 2000 you will see the General tab when you choose **File>New.**)
3. Double click your template to open it.
4. Use the worksheet to enter information.
5. When finished with the file, save it. You are not changing the template but using it to create a file based on the template.
6. Your template is still in tact and ready to be used the next time.

EDITING A TEMPLATE

1. **File>Open.**
2. Look in the template directory. This is usually inside of the Microsoft Office Folder.
3. Select your template to edit.
4. Select **Open.**
5. Make your changes.
6. **Save.**

When you open the template to make changes to it, you will need the password in order to unprotect it.

UNPROTECT THE SHEET

When you want to make changes to your worksheet design you will need to unprotect the sheet.

1. From the menu bar select **Tools>Protection> Unprotect Sheet**.
2. Type the password.
3. Select **OK**.

DELETING A TEMPLATE

1. **File>New**.
2. Select **General Templates** (In Office XP this will be in the Task Pane. In Office 2000 you will see the General tab when you choose **File>New**.)
3. Right-click the template.
4. Click **Delete**.

CREATING A TEMPLATE FOLDER

In Excel 2000 and earlier versions, a **General** template folder opens when you select **File>New**. In Excel XP, selecting **File>New** will open the task pane. On the task pane you can click **General** templates and the templates folder will open allowing you to choose a template to use.

When creating your own templates, it is wise to separate them into meaningful categories. You might choose a

"Personal" category, a "Household" category, or a category called "Sales". It does not matter how you choose to file them. What does matter is that it is meaningful to you. Just think of how you would file your templates if they were paper. Chances are you would file them in manila folders with identifying labels on each folder. This is the same idea, only you are accomplishing it electronically.

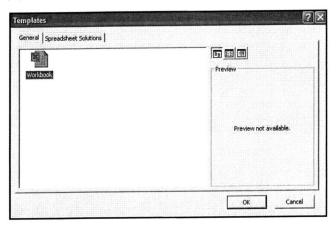

Your template filing system is developed once you have created the file that you wish to save as a template. Here's how it works.

1. Select **File>Save As**.
2. In the **Save As Type** box choose **Template**.
3. Select the **Create New Folder** icon. ⌐

4. Type the name that you want to assign the folder.
5. Select **OK**.
6. Make sure your new folder is open and that you are saving your template in your new folder.
7. Type the template name.
8. Press **Save**.

There, click by click you have created a template folder. Pretty soon you'll be helping another Excel user to create one.

When you are ready to use your template:
1. Select **File>New**.
2. Select **General Templates**.
3. Select your folder name from the tabs available.
4. Select your template.
5. Select **OK**.

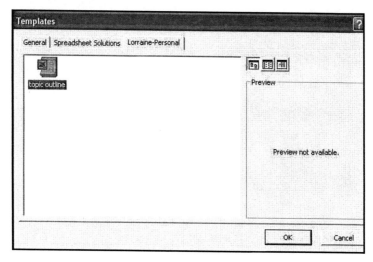

That's it for creating and using templates. You are truly becoming an expert in Excel. Keystroke-by-keystroke and click by click, you're mastering the use of Excel. Congratulations! Your commitment and stick-to-it-tiveness is paying off.

Working With Large Worksheets

*M*any of the worksheets you will use will contain several columns and many many rows. The largest I have seen was from a school district. It provided each school with a worksheet containing data on each student. The data included not only identification data such as name, grade and teacher, but it also contained gender, race, testing data for three years and much more. This worksheet contained thirty-five columns and over one-thousand rows. That's a lot of information. Actually, when a worksheet gets to be that size it may be time to consider using a relational database like Access. However, it is easier to train users on Excel. So I understand the decision to use it.

Working with a worksheet of that size presents several challenges.

- ◆ It can be difficult to read the data as you scroll to the right because the identifying information on the left disappears.

- When printing the worksheets the identifying information only prints on some of the pages.
- A data group might split between pages.
- The pages are not numbered and printed the way you would expect.
- There is just Too Much Information (TMI). What you need is a way to extract or filter it and see only what you need.

All of these are valid concerns. The first few are addressed in this chapter. For the last one, you will find using filters and pivot tables very useful. Please see the chapter *Using Excel As A Database*.

FREEZE YOUR WORKSHEET

Though this sounds like an odd term, it really makes sense. When scrolling in a large worksheet your identifying information on the far left disappears as you scroll to view the columns on the right. Likewise, your header labels up top disappear as you scroll down. Freezing the worksheet panes is a way to resolve this.

The worksheet that follows contains data for Region 1 through Region 20. If you could see the entire worksheet on your monitor, you would notice the field headings disappearing as you scroll down to see the rest of the regions. When the field headings disappear you cannot tell what month the data is for. As you scroll to the right to see the totals, the Region headings and the identifying information for each of the rows disappears. To avoid this you can freeze those row and column headings.

	March	April	May	June	July	August	September	October	November	TOTALS
I. Stephens & Associates, Onc..										
Regional Training Report Summary										
Region 1										
Word	20	6440	6009	3243	3600	4400	800	975	457	25944
Access	3240	3643	4200	4404	304	664	800	750	340	18345
Ofice	908	675	432	7890	6543	9402	722	765	986	28323
PowerPoit	4936	9234	3064	6004	340	3046	26418	1496	13402	67940
Excel	3362	4034	6423	4304	9406	4600	41775	196546	177078	447528
Region 2										
Word	3442	3942	4026	9441	9440	40030	195555	196655	186841	649373
Access	4244	4393	460	324	6494	3363	27871	19400	19115	85665
PowerPoit	44664	42004	9434	4400	6944	4609	41775	196546	177078	527456
Excel	4491	942	4470	40460	42442	44240	186582	177894	190714	692235
Ofice	908	675	432	7890	6543	9402	722	765	986	28323
Region 3										
Word	346	946	6390	3065	3440	3493	193747	193795	186310	591533
Access	3463	3094	4090	4291	464	22	18880	2043	99	36448
PowerPoit	4305	9003	3334	6344	244	3403	0	0	0	26634
Excel	3664	4406	6602	4440	9610	4433	19538	42282	19507	114482
Region 4										
Word	6495	6444	3304	4424	4024	9042	18880	2043	99	54756
Access	3634	4434	4309	4935	943	6300	21712	4151	27722	78141

Freeze row headings

1 Click in the cell directly below the row that you wish to freeze.
2. Select **Window>Freeze Panes**.

Freeze column headings

1. Click in the cell directly to the right of the column that you wish to freeze.
2. Select **Window>Freeze Panes**.

Freeze both column and row headings

1. Click in the intersecting cell that is directly to the right of the column that you wish to freeze, and below the row you wish to freeze.
2. Select **Window>Freeze Panes**.

For example, in worksheet above:
1. Clicking in A5 and freezing the panes would freeze row 4 and the rows above it.

2. Clicking in B4 and freezing the panes would freeze column A and the rows above row 4.

3. Clicking in B5 and freezing the panes would freeze everything above row 5 and column A. Thus both your column headings and your row headings would be visible as you scrolled in your worksheet.

The third choice is the one that you would want for this worksheet.

Unfreeze panes

Now suppose you want to unfreeze what you have frozen? Here's the "thaw-out" process.

1. Select **Window>Unfreeze Panes**.

PRINTING

Though you may not be able to read all of the numbers on the following pages, you can see the problems that I would like to help you avoid or resolve:

L. Stephens & Associates, Inc. Regional Training Report Summary	March	April	May	June	July	August	September	October
Region 1								
Word	20	6440	6009	3243	3600	1400	800	975
Access	3240	3643	4200	1404	304	664	800	750
Office	908	675	132	7890	6543	9402	722	765
PowerPoint	4936	9234	3064	6004	340	3046	26418	1496
Excel	3362	4034	6423	4304	9406	4600	41775	196546
Region 2								
Word	3442	3942	4026	9441	9440	40030	196555	196655
Access	4244	4393	460	324	6494	3363	27811	19400
PowerPoint	44664	42004	9434	4400	6944	4609	41775	196646
Excel	4691	942	4470	40460	42442	44240	186582	177894
Office	908	675	132	7890	6543	9402	722	765
Region 3								
Word	344	948	6390	3064	3440	3463	193747	193795
Access	3463	3094	4090	4291	464	22	18860	2043
PowerPoint	4305	9003	3334	6344	234	3463	0	0
Excel	3664	4406	6602	4440	9640	4433	19538	42282
Region 4								
Word	6495	6444	3304	4424	4024	9042	16880	2043
Access	3634	4434	4309	4935	943	6300	21742	4151
PowerPoint	40064	40304	4441	3293	963	3681	0	0
Excel	4244	420	3600	9367	44004	9694	0	0
Region 5								
Word	404	6004	6434	3447	3495	3992	18667	41030
Access	3204	3634	4444	4342	230	45	19107	1014
PowerPoint	4407	9444	3463	6443	234	3494	28361	1029
Excel	3345	4040	6532	4242	9325	4035	18667	41030
Region 6								
Word	6044	3230	3366	4036	4994	9090	28351	1029
Access	3442	4360	4633	244	6236	6306	18667	41030
PowerPoint	40824	40933	4960	3304	6325	4495	14524	27829
Excel	4404	442	4034	9494	44669	40245	41775	196546
Region 7								
Word	4004	9404	40094	44444	44494	42464	196555	196655
Access	4994	630	6464	6334	4409	4344	27811	19400
PowerPoint	43446	44243	44649	60044	4223	404	41775	196646
Excel	391	3031	40002	42405	40430	43344	186582	177894
Region 8								
Word	4449	9306	9995	44033	44044	42343	193747	193795
Access	4945	644	6400	6306	4034	4634	890	433
PowerPoint	43634	44634	44632	9944	4440	404	890	500
Excel	332	6960	40393	42330	40049	43444	700	0
Region 9								
Word	3643	4493	9033					

	Mar	Apr	May	Jun	Jul	Aug	Sep	Oct
Word	3406	3903	4490	9344	9444	40494	890	433
Access	1203	4331	440	300	6466	3306	890	500
PowerPoint	44626	44961	9403	4424	6923	4053	700	19840
Excel	4432	920	4434	40420	42366	44204	42464	186411
Region 10								
Word	4043	9044	40494	44204	44443	42090	189958	177536
Access	43	330	6024	6444	4239	4403	28339	18652
PowerPoint	43904	44302	43363	40409	4304	45	177801	18937
Excel	443	3404	40600	42945	40349	43440	189959	177536
Region 11								
Word	3643	4493	9033	40050	40043	44200	177801	18937
Access	4449	400	440	6044	3333	3430	189959	177536
PowerPoint	42443	42334	40469	6993	3894	4900	211971	19374
Excel	204	6323	9435	44006	43634	44966	0	0
Region 12								
Word	9931	44045	44390	43020	43663	44066	28351	1029
PowerPoint	430	66.30	3003	3945	9083	4441	18667	41030
Excel	66442	48606	43640	44696	9642	6333	0	0
Region 13								
Word	6044	3230	3366	4036	4994	9090	14524	27829
Access	3442	4360	4933	244	6236	6306	41775	196546
PowerPoint	40824	40933	4960	3304	6325	4495	27811	19400
Excel	4404	442	4034	9494	44069	40245	0	0
Region 14								
Word	4004	9404	40091	44444	44494	42464	41775	196546
Access	4994	630	6464	6334	4409	4344	186582	177894
PowerPoint	43446	44243	44649	40044	4223	404	195555	196655
Excel	391	3031	40092	42405	40430	43344	27811	19400
Region 15								
Word	4449	9306	9995	40033	44044	42343	186253	176217
Access	4945	644	6400	6306	4034	4634	28746	17749
PowerPoint	43634	44034	44032	9944	4440	404	437 96	19536
Excel	332	6960	42393	42330	40049	43444	186253	176217
Region 16								
Word	3408	3903	4490	9344	9444	40494	437 96	19536
PowerPoint	44626	44961	9403	4424	6923	4053	19466	30462
Excel	4432	920	4434	40420	42366	44204	9944	4440
Region 17								
Word	4043	9044	40494	44204	44443	42090	44204	44443
PowerPoint	43904	44302	43363	40409	4304	45	40409	4304
Excel	443	3404	40600	42945	40349	43440	42945	40349
Region 18								
Word	3643	4493	9033	40050	40043	44200	44204	44443

◆ The pages are not numbered.

◆ Page 1 ends with the title for Region 9 at the bottom of the page, and Page 2 has the information for Region 9 but does not have the title for Region 9.

◆ Page 2 also is missing the heading to show the months.

◆ If you would reference the picture on the previous page, you may also realize that you would prefer for the rest of the information for Region 1 through Region 8 to be your second page. It is not that way here.

What features are available to help resolve these concerns? The following respectively addresses the concerns above.

◆ Headers and Footers

◆ Page Break Preview – Controls where your page breaks occur

◆ Printing row and column headings

◆ Determining Page Order

Let's start with headers and footers. Then we will move on to the rest.

Page Headers and Footers

Headers and footers are areas above the top and bottom of the page margins. They contain information that will appear on every page. To insert headers and footers:

1. Select **File>Page Setup**.
2. Select the **Header/Footer** tab.
3. To select one of the standard headers
   a. Select the drop-down arrow next to the **Header** text box
   b. Choose from the given options
   c. Select **OK**.

4. To select one of the standard footers
   a. Select the drop-down arrow next to the **Footer** text box.
   b. Choose from the given options
   c. Select **OK**.

5. To insert a custom header or footer
   a. Click the **Custom Header** or the **Custom Footer** button
   b. Click in the left, the center or the right section to indicate which section the information will be entered into.
   c. Select the buttons to accomplish your task.
   d. Select OK.

The available buttons are described below.

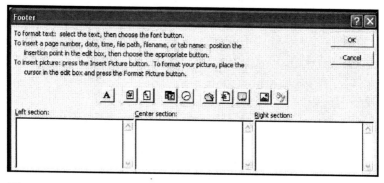

There are ten buttons on the custom header and custom footer dialog boxes. The function of each is listed in the order they appear above.

1. Format font – Select the font type, size and style that you wish for the information to appear.
2. Insert the page number.
3. Insert the number of pages.

If you wanted your page numbers to appear as **Page 1 of 3** you would follow this process:

◆ Type **Page.**
◆ Press the **space-bar.**
◆ Click the 2nd button (this will insert the page number).
◆ Press the **space-bar.**
◆ Type **of.**
◆ Press the **space-bar.**
◆ Click the 3rd button (this will insert the number of pages in the document).

4. Insert current date (This will always give the current date of printing).
5. Insert the current time (This will always give the current time of printing).
6. Insert the file name and the location of the file.
7. Insert the file name.
8. Insert the name of the sheet tab.
9. Insert a picture.
10. Format the picture that has been inserted.

Controlling page breaks

Unless you control where a page ends, Excel will create a default page break based on the paper size, font size, etc. **Page Break Preview** is a tool available to help you control where your page will break.

1. Select **View>Page Break Preview.**
2. Click **OK** if the **Welcome to Page Break Preview** dialog box opens up.
3. Increase or decrease your zoom as necessary to see your data.

4. The dotted blue lines indicate the end of your page. Drag the lines to change the beginning or ending of data on each page.

 Although you can fit more on a page by adjusting the page break, be aware that it has to scale down the page printing to make it fit. Be careful not to force too much onto a page.

Good news! You've created your own page break. Are you beginning to feel like you, not Excel, are the one in control? I hope so, because you are. Let's move on and see how to make the printed data easy to read. We can accomplish this by having the proper headings printed.

Printing row and column titles

This feature will repeat your heading row information on every page and/or your identifying column information on each page.
  1. Select **File>Page Setup**.
  2. Select the **Sheet** tab.

Print titles
  Rows to repeat at top:
  Columns to repeat at left:

3. To repeat row headings (i.e. the months in our previous example).
    a. Click in **Rows to repeat at top** in the **Print titles** section.
    b. Collapse the dialog box by clicking the red arrow.
    c. Scroll to see the row number(s) in the worksheet that you want to repeat.
    d. Select the row number(s). Notice that the Rows to repeat at top is being filled in.

e. Click the red dot to expand the dialog box.

f. Select **OK**.

4. To repeat column headings (i.e. the regions and names of courses as shown in our previous example)

a. Click in **Columns to repeat at left** in the **Print titles** section.

b. Collapse the dialog box by clicking the **red arrow**.

c. Scroll to see the column letter(s) in the worksheet that you want to repeat.

d. Select the column letter(s).

e. Click the **red dot** to expand the dialog box.

f. Select **OK**.

Presto! You're done.

Determining Page Order

By default, wide and long worksheets will print Down then Across. Thus if you document is nine pages long, the page that you expect to be page 2 may actually print as page 4. Odd? Yes, but true. However, you can control how they print.

1. Select **File>Page Setup**.

2. Select the **Sheet** tab.

3. In the **Page Order** section notice how the pages will print. Based on this example the data to the right, your worksheet will not print until all of the data in the left columns finishes printing.

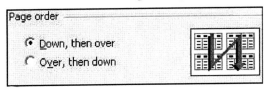

4. You can change that by selecting **Over, then down**.

 View your file in **Page Break Preview** when you make this change. You will be able to see the change immediately.

SELECTING HOW TO VIEW YOUR DATA

If your worksheet is a very wide one, you may wish to occasionally eliminate seeing some of the columns. Hiding columns is one option. The one disadvantage you may find in hiding columns is having to repetitively select them and hide or unhide them as you change your printing or viewing needs. Let me offer two features that I believe will be of benefit.

1. Grouping Data
2. Custom Views

Grouping data

When you decide to group data you are normally indicating to Excel that the selected information has something in common. Take a look at the worksheet below.

	A	B	C	D	E	F	G	H	I	J	K	L	M
1	Commerce High School												
2	Student Fund Raiser												
3													
4	Teacher	Jan	Feb	Mar	1st Qtr	Apr	May	Jun	2nd Qtr	Jul	Aug	Sep	3rd Qtr
5	Smith, S.	100	1766	300	2166	350	300	750	1400	1234	1869	2000	5103
6	Brown, N.	150	1809	700	2659	400	800	1000	2200	1765	1653	1789	5207
7	Wallace, F.	299	2195	500	2994	300	699	2000	2999	1000	2000	455	3455
8	Adams, G	199	1725	800	2724	1800	800	1500	4100	2876	1987	600	5463
9	Totals	748	7495	2300	10543	2850	2599	5250	10699	1333	7509	4844	13686

There are times when you will want to display the entire sheet, and there will be other times when you desire to show just the quarterly totals. Grouping will simplify the process.

Here is an example of this same material but grouped so that only the quarters and the annual totals show. Columns B through D, columns F through

	A	E	I	M	Q	R
1	Commerce High School					
2	Student Fund Raiser					
3						
4	Teacher	1st Qtr	2nd Qtr	3rd Qtr	4th Qtr	Annual
5	Smith, S.	2166	1400	5103	4133	12802
6	Brown, N.	2659	2200	5207	4582	14648
7	Wallace, F.	2994	2999	3455	6109	15557
8	Adams, G.	2724	4100	5463	1902	14189
9	Totals	10543	10699	19228	16726	57196
10						

H, columns J through L, and columns N through P have been grouped and are not showing.

Notice two things about this grouped worksheet:
1. There are plus symbols above the columns.
2. There is a "1" and a "2" in the upper left corner of the worksheet.

These are indicators of using grouping for your data.

You can have several levels of grouping. If columns E through Q were grouped we would have three levels. Simple right? Here's the procedure.
1. Select (highlight) the columns letters of the columns you want to group.
2. Select **Data > Group & Outline> Group**.

Showing and concealing grouped data

1. To conceal the columns that you have grouped click the **minus sign**.
2. To show the columns that you have grouped click the **plus sign**.
3. To show all of the grouped columns click the "**2**" in the upper left hand corner.
4. To conceal all of the grouped columns click the "**1**" in the upper left hand corner.

> In grouping "1" shows your highest level – usually your totals. "2" shows the next level down – usually a set of subtotals. Then "3" is used to show the next level, and "4" the next, and so on.

If you are currently asking yourself, "Is that on my computer?", the answer is "Yes." You would be surprised how often I am asked that one question.

Suppose you want to ungroup what you've grouped, to separate what you've joined, to dismantle what you've united, to ... you get the picture. Here's how.

Ungrouping data

1. Highlight the columns you wish to ungroup.
2. Select **Data > Group & Outline> Ungroup**.

> Just as we grouped the columns you could choose to group rows. The process would be the same. Select the rows that you want to group, select **Data>Group & Outline>Group**.

Custom Views

Custom views are simply different "stored" ways of looking at your information. You create custom views to avoid having to make repetitive changes to the appearance of your data when various requests are received.

As an example, several times a week you produce a printout of data. Sometimes it shows all data; sometimes it shows certain levels of grouped data; sometime it may show filtered data. [To learn more about filtered data see the chapter *Using Excel As A Database*.] If you can find a way to save the way the data looks once you create it, you will save time when someone asks to see it again. This is what **Custom Views** provides. This is a wonderful tool – try it.

- *Creating custom views* -

1. Make sure that all of your columns and rows are showing. (Not grouped or hidden).
2. Select **View>Custom Views>Add**.
3. Type **Normal** (this will be the name of your default or normal view).
4. Click **OK**.
5. Hide or group a section of your data.
6. Select **View>Custom Views> Add**.
7. Give this view a name (it is a good idea to make the name indicative of what the view shows).
8. Click **OK**.
9. Repeat this process (steps 5 through 8) until you have established the views that you want.
10. When finished select **Close**.

- *Showing Custom Views* -

1. Select **View>Custom Views**.
2. Select the name of the view you want to see.
3. Select **Show**.

- *Printing Custom Views* -

When you print your worksheet, it will print what is showing. Therefore selecting a custom view before you print will control what you are printing.

1. **View>Custom Views**.
2. Select the view that you want to print.
3. Select **Show**.
4. Select **File>Print**.

- *Deleting Custom Views* -

When you are sure you no longer need to save a custom view you may wish to delete it.

1. Select **View>Custom Views**.
2. Select the name of the custom view you wish to delete.
3. Select **Delete**.
4. Click **Yes**.
5. Click **Close**.

Summary

Hurrah! You've completed this chapter on working with large worksheets in record time. It's probably crossed your mind again that you have just uncovered some techniques that you wish you had known yesterday. There are millions of people out there today who do not know what you now know about Excel. Allow yourself to feel good about your growing level of expertise.

As we move into the next chapter on using Excel as a database, try not to forget the features covered here. Very large worksheets are often used in Excel databases.

Using Excel as a Database

*A*ctually, Excel is a database. Because of it's simplicity it is really quite a good one. A database consists of:

◆ Fields
◆ Records

In Excel a field is a column, and a record is a row. Therefore a list of information entered into a worksheet with fields and records is a database. (You may want to reread those two sentences.) Being able to manipulate the data is the key. Some of the Excel features that will assist you with data manipulation will be presented.

When I think of data manipulations the following come to mind:

◆ Sorting data
◆ Rearranging data
◆ Selecting data that meets a criteria
◆ Showing the data in chart format
◆ Performing calculations on the data
◆ And more

We will only examine some of them because I want to leave room for the rest of them in my next book. Just kidding. Seriously though, I've included the most frequently used ones in this book so you can get a head start on using Excel as a database. If the spirit moves you to want to know more about data manipulation, I'm just an e-mail or a seminar away.

SORTING RECORDS

Although entire manuals have been written on this subject, in the next few pages you'll learn enough about sorting to be quite proficient at it. Sorting consists of arranging a list alphabetically, numerically, or in some preferred sequence.

Sorting by one field

1. Click any one cell in the column that you wish to sort.
2. Select the sort icon on the toolbar. The AZ button sorts in ascending sequence. The ZA button sorts in descending sequence.

Do not highlight any data before you perform your sort. If you do, only the highlighted data will sort. This will mix up the data in your database. Bummer, right? So make sure not to do it!

Sorting by multiple fields

If you have a list that contains first name, last name, address, city, state and zip code, you have several sort options. You may wish to keep all of a zip code together, then keep all of the last names together, then within that list

sort them by first name. This is considered sorting by multiple fields. Here's how to do it.

1. Click anywhere in the list of data.
2. Select **Data>Sort**.
3. Under **Sort By** select the drop-down arrow and choose your primary sort field.
4. Choose the sequence (ascending or descending).
5. Under **Then By** select the drop-down arrow and choose your secondary sort field.
6. Choose the sequence (ascending or descending).
7. Under the second **Then By** select the drop-down arrow and choose your third sort field (if you have one).
8. Indicate if you have a **Header Row** by clicking the Header Row option under the **My List Has** area.
9. Select **OK**.

Sorting Horizontally (Reordering columns)

One of the major considerations when deciding what sequence you will use to list your fields is the knowledge of how you will receive the data. If you are expecting the information to be given to you on a form that has the information in the sequence of First Name, Last Name, Department, and City of residence, you would design your worksheet with the fields listed in this order. If not, you will have to tab around too much to enter the data.

In spite of all of the careful planning that you do, someone (you probably know who they are) is going to give you a stack of information that is in a different order. Not to worry! You can rearrange the fields of your database as many times as you wish and never loose your data. Here's how you accomplish that.

Using this worksheet as the example:

	A	B	C	D
4				
5	**First Name**	**Last Name**	**Department**	**City**
6	Doris	Tyson	Sales	Raleigh
7	Barbara	Burns	Technology	New York
8	Tanya	Carr	Administration	Brooklyn
9	Therman	Jackson	Sales	Ashville
10	John	McPhee	Advertising	Yancyville
11	Charles	Forsythe	Administration	Detroit
12	Carolyn	Rooks	Technology	Newberry
13	Myra	Brown	Human Resources	Columbia
14	Ed	Reynolds	Technology	White Plains
15	Doris	Rooks	Sales	Las Vegas

You are prepared to enter data that will be given to you in this sequence. But what do you do if the data comes from different people in different sequences? What do you do if the information one person gives has the information in the following sequence:

♦ Department
♦ Last Name
♦ First Name
♦ City

To make data entry easy, I recommend you rearrange your columns by sorting horizontally. To do so, simply follow these procedures.

1. Make sure there is a blank row above your column headings.
2. In that blank row, number your columns in the sequence that you want them to appear.

	A	B	C	D
4	3	2	1	4
5	**First Name**	**Last Name**	**Department**	**City**
6	Doris	Tyson	Sales	Raleigh
7	Barbara	Burns	Technology	New York
8	Tanya	Carr	Administration	Brooklyn
9	Therman	Jackson	Sales	Ashville
10	John	McPhee	Advertising	Yancyville
11	Charles	Forsythe	Administration	Detroit
12	Carolyn	Rooks	Technology	Newberry
13	Myra	Brown	Human Resources	Columbia
14	Ed	Reynolds	Technology	White Plains
15	Doris	Rooks	Sales	Las Vegas

3. Click in the list, then click **Data>Sort>Options**.
4. On the **Sort Options** dialog box select **Sort left to right**.
5. Click **OK**.
6. Click **OK**.

Good job. You're done.

 This might be a good time to go back to the sort options window and reset the Sort top to bottom. Otherwise you might get some strange results on your next sort.

 Be sure there is a bank row above the numbers that you type in to determine the field sequence.

Custom Sort Orders

Sorts naturally happen in this order:

◆ Numbers are sorted from the smallest negative number to the largest positive number.

◆ Dates and times are sorted based on their value.

◆ Text (and text that includes numbers) is sorted as follows: 0 1 2 3 4 5 6 7 8 9 (space) ! " # $ % & ' ( ) * + , - . / : ; < = > ? @ [\ ] ^ _ ` { | } ~ A B C D E F G H I J K L M N O P Q R S T U V W X Y Z.

◆ Blanks are sorted last.

Thus if you were sorting the information in the department row in ascending order, it would return with Administration first, followed by Advertising, followed by Human Resources, then Sales, then finally Technology. However, your desire might be for your records to sort in this manner:

- ◆ Sales
- ◆ Human Resources
- ◆ Technology
- ◆ Advertising
- ◆ Administration

In order to accomplish this you will want to define a custom sort.

- Defining a custom sort list -

As usual, there is more than one way to define the custom sort order. Since you are such a devoted reader, I will demonstrate my preferred method.

1. Type your list somewhere on your worksheet. (Anywhere is fine. This is just temporary.) Be sure to enter your list in the order that you would like to see the items sorted. Each entry in its own cell. If we were following the example above, we would have five cells with information in them.
2. Highlight the cells.
3. Select **Tools>Options>**Select the **Custom Lists** tab.
4. The lower right hand corner will contain the address of the cells that have your list typed into them.
5. Select **Import>OK**.

 Once you have imported the list you can erase that area of the worksheet. It was only used for the import.

- Using your custom list for sorting -

When you are ready to perform a sort on the fields that you have defined a special sort order for, follow these procedures.

1. Click in the list. (Do not highlight parts of your list. Let the system choose the entire list).
2. From the menu bar select **Data>Sort>Options**.
3. Click the drop-down arrow under **First key sort order**.
4. Choose your custom sort order.
5. Select **OK**.
6. Select your primary field to sort by from the **Sort by** drop-down arrow.
7. Choose ascending or descending.
8. Select your second and third fields to sort by (if you are doing a multiple sort). Remember to choose ascending or descending.
9. Click **Header Row** to indicate that your list has a header row.
10. Select **OK**.

 Don't forget to go back to the sort options and reset the **First Key Sort Order** to normal before your next sort.

 If the time should come that you no longer need to use the custom list, you should delete it. **Tools>Options>Custom List** tab. Select the one to delete>Press **Delete**.

TRANSPOSE — SWITCH ROWS TO COLUMNS & COLUMNS TO ROWS

I'll bet you really do wish you had known this one yesterday. I have seen a lot of copying and pasting whenever someone has wanted to switch the positioning of the row headings with the column headings. You'll be amazed at how easy this is once you instruct Excel to do the work.

Example – Switching your rows and columns

You have entered the data into your worksheet listing grades 1 through 12 in row 1, as seen in #1 below. (To save space I have only entered grades 1 and 2, but it will suffice to demonstrate how **Transpose** works.) You then realize that the sheet will be too wide and decide you would rather have the grades listed in a column, and the other fields listed in a row (as seen in #2 below).

#1

	A	B	C
1		1st grade	2nd grade
2	Name	Lorraine	Mildred
3	Address	527 West 143rd Street	444 Met Oval
4	City	New York	Bronx

#2

	A	B	C	D	E	F
1		Name	Address	City	State	Zip
2	1st grade	Lorraine	527 West 143rd Street	New York	NY	10031
3	2nd grade	Mildred	444 Met Oval	Bronx	NY	10461

How do you take all of the data that you have entered and reverse it? The answer, dear reader, is **Transpose**. Here is how it works.

1. Highlight the data that you wish to rearrange. In the #1 worksheet above it would be A1:C4.
2. Select **Copy**.
3. Right-click in a blank cell where you want your rearranged data to appear.
4. Select **Paste Special>Transpose>OK**.

It just couldn't be easier!

 When you select the beginning cell for pasting, be sure you have enough space to paste the transposed data. If you do not it will overlay any existing data.

If it is time for another stretch break, roll your shoulders, rotate your neck, relax, wiggle your fingers, and grab something refreshing. I bet you wish you had done that five minutes ago. When you are ready, let's take a peek at filtering records.

FILTERING RECORDS

Filtering simply means selecting specific records based on the criteria that you assign. If you had a list of every member of your church and wanted to form a Singles Ministry, using the filter feature would allow you to select any member with a status of "Single". Though there are many ways of filtering we will examine three.

◆ AutoFilter
◆ Advanced filter
◆ Forms

AutoFilter

AutoFilter allows you to very easily select data to display. First you must enable the AutoFilter feature. From that point on, it is very easy.

- Enable AutoFilter -

1. Select any cell in your list of data.
2. Select **Data>Filter >Autofilter**.
3. Notice that each field heading now has drop-down arrows on the right side.

- Use AutoFilter -

To filter records simply select the drop-down arrow next to the field. For example:

To choose all members of the sales department:

1. Select the Drop-down arrow next to Department.
2. Choose **Sales**.
3. Your filtered list appears in the place of the long list that was there.

	A	B	C
1	First Name ▼	Last Name ▼	Department ▼
2	Doris	Tyson	Sales
3	Barbara	Burns	Technology
4	Tanya	Carr	Administration
5	Therman	Jackson	Sales
6	John	McPhee	Advertising
7	Charles	Forsythe	Administration
8	Carolyn	Rooks	Technology
9	Myra	Brown	Human Resources
10	Ed	Reynolds	Technology
11	Doris	Walker	Sales
12			

4. The number of selected records is found in the status bar (bottom left side of screen).
5. A blue drop-down arrow indicates that a filter was applied to that field.

If you wish to filter another field, simply follow the same procedure. Click the drop-down arrow and make your choice. Now suppose you want to make a few comparisons. The Custom feature of Autofilter allows you to accomplish this.

- Custom AutoFilter -

Custom AutoFilters allow you use comparisons such as greater than, less than, not equal to, etc. In the above example if you wanted to select everyone that is not in the sales department, follow this process.

1. Select the Drop-down arrow for the Department field.
2. Select **Custom**.
3. On the left side select **Not Equal To**.
4. In the text box on the right select **Sales**.

5. If you wish to test for an AND or an OR condition click on the appropriate choice then make the second test on that field.

6. Select **OK**.

- Removing the filter from a field -

1. Select the blue arrow(s).
2. Select **All**.

- Remove all filters -

1. Select **Data** from the menu bar.
2. Select **Filter>Show All**.

- Disabling AutoFilter -

1. Select **Data>Filter>AutoFilter**.

Advanced Filters

One of the main advantages that Advanced Filters offers you is the ability to leave the original list in tact, and place the selected records someplace else on your worksheet. Advanced Filters require two things:

- ◆ Your data list – the data that you are going to filter
- ◆ A criteria range – an area that list your criteria or choices for selection.

The criteria range must have two or more rows. The first row gives the criteria labels (which are the same labels shown in your list). It is very important that this row is spelled exactly like your original data labels. For this reason I recommend that you copy the labels and paste them into a criteria row. The second row contains the conditions that you are testing for. This may seem a bit technical at first, but let's look at it.

- Enabling Advanced Filters -

1. Copy the heading row and paste it in a row anywhere on your worksheet.

	A	B	C
1	First Name	Last Name	Department
2		Rooks	
3			
4			
5	First Name	Last Name	Department
6	Doris	Tyson	Sales
7	Barbara	Burns	Technology
8	Tanya	Carr	Administration
9	Therman	Jackson	Sales
10	John	McPhee	Advertising
11	Charles	Forsythe	Administration
12	Carolyn	Rooks	Technology
13	Myra	Brown	Human Resources
14	Ed	Reynolds	Technology
15	Doris	Rooks	Sales

2. Type the criteria that you are filtering for under the appropriate filed name.

3. If there is more than one criterion required for a match, type it on the same row. (i.e. if the department is sales and the last name is Rooks, type this on the same row). This creates an **AND** condition for the criteria.

4. If there is an **OR** condition (i.e. if the department is sales or if the department is technology), the second set of criteria goes on the next row. If there is a third **OR** condition it goes on the next row. (By now you've gathered that each **OR** set of conditions will go on its own row. You are beginning to think like an Excel pro.)

5. Make sure to leave at least one blank row between the criteria and the data that you are analyzing.

You can use comparison criteria to enter criteria.	
= Equal to	< Less than
<= Less than or equal to	> Greater than
>= Greater than or equal to	<> Not equal to

You can also use wild cards (i.e. asterisks, question marks, etc.) to enter your criteria. A criteria of "ad*" under a field name would search for everything that started with "ad". A criteria of "*ad*" would search the field for all occurrences of "ad" anywhere in the field.

- Using Advanced Filters -

As with AutoFilters you are able to filter the list and see the selected records (commonly called the *record set*) instead of the entire list. Advanced Filters, however, offer the ability for you to filter the list and save the record set in a different place on the worksheet. This feature allows you to create several lists of selected records and save them for printing. It eliminates the need to re-filter every time the same request is made. This is such a neat feature. While you're in the mood, let's tackle an example using Advanced Filter.

 Record Set – a list of records that match the defined criteria

Example - Advanced filters – filter in place

Very much like AutoFilter, this will filter a list and hide all records that do not match the criteria.

1. Enter your criteria in the criteria row(s). Be sure that you have already placed your criteria labels in the first of the criteria rows.

2. Take note of the range of your criteria fields. In the example shown it starts in A1 and ends in C2. The address of the first field name and the address of the last cell where your criteria could be defined.

3. Click anywhere in the data list.

4. In the menu bar select **Data>Filter>Advanced Filter**.

5. The **Advanced Filter** dialog box will appear. Because you clicked in the data list before selecting **Advanced Filter,** the List range is already completed.

6. Click in the **Criteria range** text box. Click the red arrow to the right of the text box to collapse the dia-

log box enabling you to see your criteria range in your worksheet.

7. Highlight the entire criteria range (A1:C2)
8. Click the red arrow to the right of the text box again and expand the dialog box.
9. The List range and the Criteria range are now filled in.
10. By default the **Filter the list in place** button is selected. Leave it that way.
11. Select **OK**.

Voila! You're done.

Let's try another example while you are on a roll.

Example - Advanced Filters – Copy to another location

1. Enter your criteria in the criteria row(s). Be sure that you have already placed your criteria labels in the first of the criteria rows.
2. Take note of the range of your criteria fields. In the example shown, it starts in A1 and ends in C2. The address of the first field name and the address of the last possible criteria.
3. Decide where on your worksheet you want your filtered list to appear. Be careful and do not decide to place it where it may overlay other data.
4. Click anywhere in the data list.
5. In the menu bar select **Data>Filter>Advanced Filter**.
6. The Advanced Filter dialog box will appear. Because you clicked in the data list before selecting Advanced Filter the **List range** is already completed.
7. If the **Criteria range** text box is not already filled in correctly:

    a. Click in the **Criteria range** text box.

    b. Click the red arrow to the right of the text box to collapse the dialog box enabling you to see your criteria range in your work sheet.

    c. Highlight the entire criteria range.

    d. Click the red arrow to the right of the text box again and expand the dialog box.

8. The **List range** and the **Criteria range** are now filled in.

9. Select the **Copy to another location** option found at the top of the dialog box.

10. Notice that a third text box opened. Here you will indicate the starting location where your filtered list will appear.

    a. Click in the **Copy to another location** text box.

    b. Click the **red arrow** to the right of the text box to collapse the dialog box enabling you to see your worksheet.

    c. Click in the cell where the beginning of your filtered data will be written.

    d. Click the red arrow to the right of the text box again and expand the dialog box.

11. Select **OK**.

The data matching the criteria you defined should be listed in a new location in your worksheet. Your original data is in its same location – undisturbed. (What a smart program, and it's totally devoted toward making your life easier. If no one is looking, feel free to give your computer a gentle pat on the top or kiss the display. Show it a little love for being such a labor saving device.)

 One word of caution. As you change the number of OR conditions the number of rows defining your criteria range will change. Be sure to check the criteria range field each time to verify that you are looking at the correct range. A common error is to leave an extra row in the criteria range when the number of OR conditions is reduced. This will create invalid results when you apply your filter.

Filtering With Forms

If you have read the chapter *What is Microsoft Excel?*, you saw how using forms can enhance entering data. You can also use forms to select or filter records. Unlike Autofilter or Advanced Filter, forms will only show you one record at a time.

1. Click any cell in the data list.
2. Select **Data>Form**.
3. Click the **Criteria** button.
4. Type your criteria into the various fields.
5. Click **Find Next** and/or **Find Previous** until you have stepped through your list showing the records that meet your criteria.
6. When finished, click **Close**.

SUMMARIZING DATA

You have several methods available to summarize data. The choice that you make will depend on how you want to display the information and what you are looking for. We will examine three of those methods.

1. Subtotals
2. Pivot Tables
3. Conditional Sums

For the examples in this section, we will use the following data:

	A	B	C	D	E	F	G	H	I
1	SCHL	GD	Last Name	First Name	Race	Gender	Reading Score 2000	Reading Score 2001	Change in Score
2	111	6	Green	Tiffany	Asia	F	3.0	4.0	1.0
3	100	6	McPhee	Ray	Asia	M	3.0	3.0	0.0
4	112	5	Rooks	Thomas	Asia	M	2.0	3.0	1.0
5	112	7	Allen	Dorrian	BLCK	M	2.0	3.0	1.0
6	111	7	Stephens	Tressie	BLCK	F	4.0	3.0	-1.0
7	111	7	Jackson	Earlene	BLCK	F	1.0	3.0	2.0
8	111	7	Reynolds	Lois	BLCK	F	2.0	4.0	2.0
9	111	5	Warrior	Lonnette	BLCK	F	2.0	3.0	1.0
10	111	7	Rooks	Takara	Multi	F	1.0	2.0	1.0
11	112	5	Hines	Yvonna	Multi	F	3.0	3.0	0.0
12	111	5	Gilliam	Carolyn	Multi	F	2.0	2.0	0.0
13	111	6	Brown	Lorraine	WHTE	F	2.0	2.0	0.0
14	111	5	Wood	Ellie	WHTE	F	3.5	3.0	-0.5
15	111	5	Tyson	Yvonne	Multi	F	2.5	4.0	1.5
16	111	5	Watkins	Anna	WHTE	F	2.5	2.5	0.0
17	111	5	James	Thomasina	WHTE	F	2.0	4.0	2.0
18	111	6	Allen	Bill	WHTE	M	2.0	2.0	0.0
19	111	7	Green	Laura	Multi	F	2.5	4.0	1.5
20	100	5	Wise	Eddie	WHTE	M	3.0	3.0	0.0

Subtotals

This feature allows you to easily calculate grand totals and subtotals of your data.

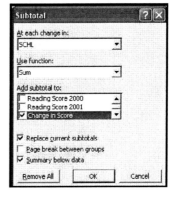

1. Sort the list by the column for which you want to calculate subtotals.
2. Click any cell in the list.
3. On the menu bar select **Data>Subtotals**.
4. In the **At each change in** box, choose the field that contains the groups for which you want subtotals.
5. In the **Use function** box, click the function you want to use to calculate the subtotals.
6. In the **Add subtotal to** box, select the check box(es) for the columns that you wish to subtotal.
7. Select **OK**.

That's all there is to it. Now let's see how it works.

Example

Using the same data, we want to calculate the average of the "Change in Score" for each school. This is found in column I.

1. Sort the list by school number.
2. Click any cell in the list.
3. On the menu bar select **Data>Subtotals**.
4. In the *At each change in* box, select SCHL.
5. In the **Use Function** box choose **Average**.
6. In the **Add subtotals to** box select **Change in Score**.
7. Select **OK**.

	SCHL	GD	Last Name	First Name	Race	Gender	Reading Score 2000	Reading Score 2001	Change in Score
1									
2	100	6	McPhee	Ray	Asia	M	3.0	3.0	0.0
3	100	5	Wise	Eddie	WHTE	M	3.0	3.0	0.0
4	100 Average								0.0
5	111	6	Green	Tiffany	Asia	F	3.0	4.0	1.0
6	111	7	Stephens	Tressie	BLCK	F	4.0	3.0	-1.0
7	111	7	Jackson	Earlene	BLCK	F	1.0	3.0	2.0
8	111	7	Reynolds	Lois	BLCK	F	2.0	4.0	2.0
9	111	5	Warrior	Lonnette	BLCK	F	2.0	3.0	1.0
10	111	7	Rooks	Takara	Multi	F	1.0	2.0	1.0
11	111	5	Gilliam	Carolyn	Multi	F	2.0	2.0	0.0
12	111	6	Brown	Lorraine	WHTE	F	2.0	2.0	0.0
13	111	5	Wood	Ellie	WHTE	F	3.5	3.0	-0.5
14	111	5	Tyson	Yvonne	Multi	F	2.5	4.0	1.5
15	111	5	Watkins	Anna	WHTE	F	2.5	2.5	0.0
16	111	5	James	Thomasina	WHTE	F	2.0	4.0	2.0
17	111	6	Allen	Bill	WHTE	M	2.0	2.0	0.0
18	111	7	Green	Laura	Multi	F	2.5	4.0	1.5
19	111 Average								0.8
20	112	5	Rooks	Thomas	Asia	M	2.0	3.0	1.0
21	112	7	Allen	Dorrian	BLCK	M	2.0	3.0	1.0
22	112	5	Hines	Yvonna	Multi	F	3.0	3.0	0.0
23	112 Average								0.7
24	Grand Average								0.7

You see three levels of information. This is very much like grouping. In the upper left corner

♦ Click 1 to show the Average for all of the schools combined.
♦ Click 2 to show the Average for each school.
♦ Click 3 to see all of the detail records.

PivotTables

What is a PivotTable? Though the name may sound confusing, it begins to make sense when you examine the words separately.

◆ Table – a method of organizing data into rows and columns for ease of legibility

◆ Pivot – Turn around; spin

Putting them together, we begin to understand that these are tables that are not stagnant, but ones that we can turn around and look at in various ways. A regular table is two-dimensional. PivotTables can express data in three dimensions.

Let this section serve as an introduction to using pivot tables. The topic is so broad that it could take the entire book to cover. However, after reading this section you will be able to understand the basics and begin to apply them to analyzing your data. Okay, let's create a PivotTable.

- Creating a PivotTable -

1. Click any cell in the list or database.
2. Select **Data>PivotTable /Pivot Chart Report**.
3. A PivotTable wizard will appear to step you through the process in three steps
   a. Step 1
      i. Select Microsoft Excel list or database.
      ii. Select PivotTable.
      iii. Select Next.
   b. Step 2
      i. Verify that the data range that you are gong to work with is correct. If it is not correct collapse the dialog box and highlight the correct range.
      ii. Select Next.
   c. Step 3

    i. Select Layout.

    ii. Drag the field(s) that will be your row heading into the Row area.

    iii. Drag the field(s) that will be your column heading into the Column area.

    iv. Drag the field(s) that will be your page heading into the Page area.

    v. Drag the field(s) that will contain your calculations into the Data area.

    vi. Select OK.

  d. Select Finish.

Now let's try an example.

Example

As a "school administrator" you have the responsibility of analyzing data regarding your students and their performance. One of the things that you wish to know is the number of students that you have by gender and by race. Possibly you will want a breakdown by grade level, so why not set up the pivot table to provide all of these requests.

We will use the data in the worksheet that follows.

	A	B	C	D	E	F	G	H	I
1	SCHL	GD	Last Name	First Name	Race	Gender	Reading Score 2000	Reading Score 2001	Change in Score
2	100	6	McPhee	Ray	Asia	M	3.0	3.0	0.0
3	100	5	Wise	Eddie	WHTE	M	3.0	3.0	0.0
4	111	6	Green	Tiffany	Asia	F	3.0	4.0	1.0
5	111	7	Stephens	Tressie	BLCK	F	4.0	3.0	-1.0
6	111	7	Jackson	Earlene	BLCK	F	1.0	3.0	2.0
7	111	7	Reynolds	Lois	BLCK	F	2.0	4.0	2.0
8	111	5	Warrior	Lonnette	BLCK	F	2.0	3.0	1.0
9	111	7	Rooks	Takara	Multi	F	1.0	2.0	1.0
10	111	5	Gilliam	Carolyn	Multi	F	2.0	2.0	0.0
11	111	6	Brown	Lorraine	WHTE	F	2.0	2.0	0.0
12	111	5	Wood	Ellie	WHTE	F	3.5	3.0	-0.5
13	111	5	Tyson	Yvonne	Multi	F	2.5	4.0	1.5
14	111	5	Watkins	Anna	WHTE	F	2.5	2.5	0.0
15	111	5	James	Thomasina	WHTE	F	2.0	4.0	2.0
16	111	6	Allen	Bill	WHTE	M	2.0	2.0	0.0
17	111	7	Green	Laura	Multi	F	2.5	4.0	1.5
18	112	5	Rooks	Thomas	Asia	M	2.0	3.0	1.0
19	112	7	Allen	Dorrian	BLCK	M	2.0	3.0	1.0
20	112	5	Hines	Yvonna	Multi	F	3.0	3.0	0.0

This is a lengthy procedure, so take your time.

1. Click any cell in the list or database.
2. Select **Data>PivotTable /Pivot Chart Report**.
3. A PivotTable wizard will appear to step you through the process in three steps
   a. Step 1
      i. Select **Microsoft Excel** list or database.
      ii. Select **PivotTable**.
      iii. Select **Next**.
   b. Step 2
      i. Verify that the data range that you are gong to work with is correct. If it is not correct collapse the dialog box and highlight the correct range.
      ii. Select **Next**.
      iii. If you already have one pivot table in your workbook, you will be asked if you want to save memory by replacing it rather than creating another one. Until you have a feel for which ones you want to keep, let's just say **No**.
   c. Step 3
      i. Select **Layout**.
      ii. Drag GD over and drop it in the **Page** field in the layout.
      iii. Drag Race over and place it in the **Row** field of the layout.

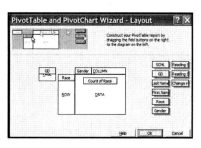

      iv. Drag Gender over and place it in the **Column** field of the layout.

    v. In this example it will not matter if you count
       race or gender, so I will drag race over to the
       data area.
    vi. Select **OK**.
   vii. Select **New worksheet** for the placement of
       your PivotTable.
   viii. Select Finish.

This is our PivotTable and it shows many things. Among
them are:

- There are 19 students that are in the school.
- 3 of them are Asian, 5 are Black, 5 are Multi
  Cultural, 6 are White.
- It also tells the number of each by gender.
- Notice that Race, Gender and GD have drop-
  down arrows. From our discussion on filters, we
  know this means we can select to view only certain records.

	A	B	C	D
1	GD	(All) ▾		
2				
3	Count of Race	Gender ▾		
4	Race ▾	F	M	Grand Total
5	Asia	1	2	3
6	BLCK	4	1	5
7	Multi	5		5
8	WHTE	4	2	6
9	Grand Total	14	5	19

For this example let's ask for only the 5th grade. We will do
this by selecting the drop-down arrow for GD. Right now
we all looking at **All** grades.

1. Select the drop-down arrow for GD found up top in
   the **Page** area.
2. Select the fifth grade students by clicking 5. Click
   OK.

3. The data shown now changes to display only the 5th grade students. Look in the GD area to see the grade that is being displayed is 5.

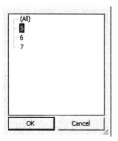

	A	B	C	D
1	GD	5 ▼		
2				
3	Count of Race	Gender ▼		
4	Race ▼	F	M	Grand Total
5	Asia		1	1
6	BLCK	1		1
7	Multi	3		3
8	WHTE	3	1	4
9	Grand Total	7	2	9

4. If you only wanted 5th grade females- then select Gender and choose Female.
5. If you only wanted 5th grade females that were Multicultural, then select the drop down arrow for Race and choose Multicultural in addition to choosing female for gender and 5th for grade.

Seeing this data in this format is wonderful, isn't it? But since you are a genuinely devoted, student-centered school administrator, you want to know the details behind these numbers. Who are the three female Multicultural students that appear in this report?

- Seeing the detail of the data displayed -

1. Double click the number that you want to see the detail for.
2. A separate worksheet will be displayed listing the names of each of the students .

	A	B	C	D	E	F	G	H	I
1	SCHL	GD	Last Name	First Name	Race	Gender	Reading Score 2000	Reading Score 2001	Change in Score
2	112	5	Hines	Yvonna	Multi	F	3	3	0
3	111	5	Tyson	Yvonne	Multi	F	2.5	4	1.5
4	111	5	Gilliam	Carolyn	Multi	F	2	2	0

- Displaying your PivotTable data as a chart -

As discussed earlier, a picture is worth a thousand words. Being able to display a pivot table as a chart gives you a chart that is just as interactive as the pivot table. (That's my story and I'm sticking to it.)

1. Click any cell in the pivot table.
2. Press **F11**.
3. Format the chart using the right-click, double-click or **Format Chart Object** button on the toolbar.
4. Use the drop-down arrows on the chart to filter data.

 The data area is the only area that must have information. The others (row and column headings) are required to create meaningful PivotTables but you can create one without them.

If you create another pivot table when one already exists in the workbook, Excel will ask if you want to replace the existing one and save memory. If you say "Yes" it will delete your existing one and replace it with the new one. If you want to keep the old one and add the new one, click "No".

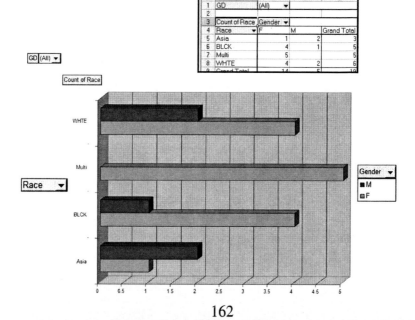

Notice that the chart also has drop-down arrows. This will allow you to filter the data just like the table did.

- Modifying a PivotTable -

You can pivot your pivot table to show the data a different way. Simply drag the field names from the row and place them on the column, and/or from the grade to the column. You see, you arrange, or pivot, the data in any way that you want. Take a look at the picture below. When you change your pivot table to look like the layout on the left, you receive the results on the right.

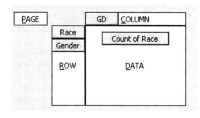

Notice:
- Both race and gender are in the row area
- Grade is in the column area
- Count of race is still in the data area

The following picture shows the parts you need when working with PivotTables. In Office 2000 the Pivot Table Field List will look a little different, but there is not very much of a difference in creating the PivotTable. Both have the field list, the layout area, and the pivot table toolbar.

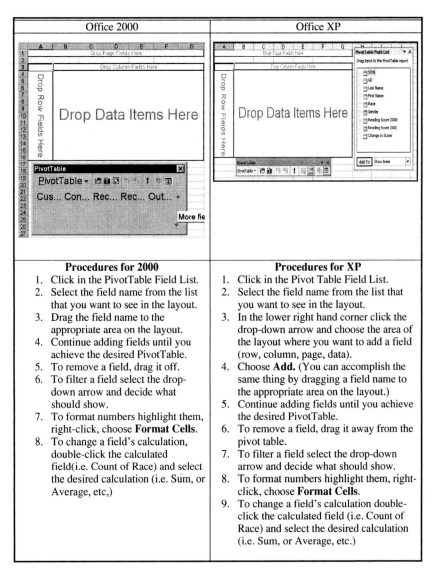

Office 2000	Office XP

Procedures for 2000

1. Click in the PivotTable Field List.
2. Select the field name from the list that you want to see in the layout.
3. Drag the field name to the appropriate area on the layout.
4. Continue adding fields until you achieve the desired PivotTable.
5. To remove a field, drag it off.
6. To filter a field select the drop-down arrow and decide what should show.
7. To format numbers highlight them, right-click, choose **Format Cells**.
8. To change a field's calculation, double-click the calculated field(i.e. Count of Race) and select the desired calculation (i.e. Sum, or Average, etc,)

Procedures for XP

1. Click in the Pivot Table Field List.
2. Select the field name from the list that you want to see in the layout.
3. In the lower right hand corner click the drop-down arrow and choose the area of the layout where you want to add a field (row, column, page, data).
4. Choose **Add**. (You can accomplish the same thing by dragging a field name to the appropriate area on the layout.)
5. Continue adding fields until you achieve the desired PivotTable.
6. To remove a field, drag it away from the pivot table.
7. To filter a field select the drop-down arrow and decide what should show.
8. To format numbers highlight them, right-click, choose **Format Cells**.
9. To change a field's calculation double-click the calculated field (i.e. Count of Race) and select the desired calculation (i.e. Sum, or Average, etc.)

Just don't give up what you're trying to do.
Where there is Love and inspiration, I
don't think you can go wrong.
Ella Fitzgerald, American singer

Conditional Sums

When you need to summarize values in your database list based on specific conditions, you will find the **Conditional Sum Wizard** a handy tool.

The Conditional Sum Wizard is not a part of the standard installation. If you do not see it under Tools then add it in.
1. **Tools>Add Ins**>Check the **Conditional Sum Wizard>OK**.

Here is how you put the wizard to work.
1. Click **Tools>Conditional Sum**.
2. The Conditional Sum Wizard starts with step 1 – verify the data range.
3. Select **Next**.
4. Select the column to sum from the drop-down list in **Column to sum**.
5. Define the criteria that you want to test for – Column, condition, and value.
6. Select **Add Condition**.
7. Continue defining the other criteria and selecting **Add Condition** until all of your conditions have been listed.
8. Click **Next**.
9. Your answers will appear in a window.
10. Decide whether to print just the answer, or the answer and the criteria.

Example

Find the total sales for sales made to SilverSmith by Alexander. Save the answer and the criteria in cells A16:C16.

We will use this worksheet for our example.

Rep	Customer	JAN	FEB	MAR	QTR 1	APR	MAY	JUN
Alexander	SilverSmith	8,751.60	9,003.15	7,378.80	25,133.55	6,341.40	5,211.38	3,457.35
Alexander	SilverSmith	10,627.94	10,933.43	8,960.81	30,522.18	7,701.00	6,328.69	4,198.61
Alexander	Focus V	13,816.33	14,213.45	11,649.06	39,678.84	10,011.30	8,227.30	5,458.19
Carson	Focus V	7,182.50	7,982.00	8,526.70	23,691.20	9,415.90	9,880.00	10,530.00
Carson	St. David	5,451.52	6,058.34	6,471.77	17,981.62	7,146.67	7,498.92	7,992.27
Carson	St. Paul	7,156.43	7,953.02	8,495.75	23,605.19	9,381.72	9,844.13	10,491.77
Carson	St. David	3,163.88	3,594.83	4,095.00	10,853.70	4,290.98	5,168.48	5,522.40
Carson	Times, Inc	3,842.21	4,365.56	4,972.97	13,180.73	5,210.96	6,276.60	6,706.40
Carson	SilverSmith	4,994.87	5,675.22	6,464.86	17,134.95	6,774.25	8,159.57	8,718.32
Falcon	Times, Inc	11,668.80	12,004.20	9,838.40	33,511.40	8,455.20	6,948.50	4,609.80
Falcon	Times, Inc	8,856.62	9,111.19	7,467.35	25,435.15	6,417.50	5,273.91	3,498.84
Falcon	SilverSmith	11,626.44	11,960.62	9,802.68	33,389.74	8,424.50	6,923.27	4,593.06

1. Click in the data.
2. Select **Tools>Conditional Sum**.
3. Select **Next**.
4. You will now see the dialog box as shown for Step 2 of 4.
5. For **Column to sum**, select **Total**.
6. Choose the following values:

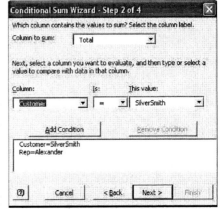

Column	Is	This value
Rep	=	Alexander

7. Select **Add**.

Column	Is	This value
Customer	=	SilverSmith

8. Select **Add**.
9. Select **Next**.
10. You will now see the dialog box for Step 3 of 4. The answers are shown here.

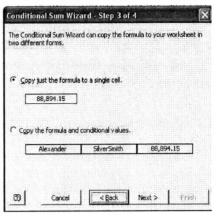

11. Choose to **Copy the formula and conditional values**.
12. Select **Next**.

13. Select **display the answer and the conditional values**.
14. Click **Next**.
15. Click in **A16**.
16. Click **Next**.
17. Click in **B16**.
18. Click **Next**.
19. Click in **C16**.
20. Click **Finish**.
21. This is the answer that is entered in A16:C16.

	A	B	C
5			
6	Alexander	SilverSmith	88,894.15

USING DATABASE FUNCTIONS

To demonstrate the Database functions, we will use the database on the following page. The first example will be covered in depth. The rest will be covered in less detail. Why? Once you have an understanding of how one of the Database functions work, I believe you will be able to understand the others. (How's that for a vote of confidence?)

When you are working with a criteria area there are a few points to remember:
1. **AND** conditions are entered on the same row.
2. **OR** conditions are entered on a separate row.

Look for these in the examples that follow if they are based on **Criteria**.

There are three ways of entering these formulas. The difference in the way you enter it will depend on how you choose to enter the reference to the criteria. In order for you to see all three, the first two examples are demonstrated showing all options.

	A	B	C	
1	**Department**	**Manager**	**Salary**	} *Criteria*
2				*area*
3				
4				
5	**Department**	**Manager**	**Salary**	
6	Research	M. Stokes	$86,000	
7	Sales	B. Peterson	$91,000	
8	Development	S. Dozier	$79,000	
9	Marketing	I. Moore	$81,000	
10	Advertising	D. Stephens	$95,000	} *Database*
11	Marketing	T. Stephens	$94,000	*list*
12	Marketing	L. Green	$97,000	
13	Development	E. Green	$97,000	
14	Research	R. Doctor	$82,000	
15				
16		Database average		

Examples
Average – DAVERAGE
Example 1: Find the average salary of managers in the database
$$=DAVERAGE(database, field, criteria)$$

Our field is salary. We do not have any criteria defined since we are averaging all of the salaries.

1. Select the cell that will contain your formula.
2. Type any of the following formulas.

$$=DAVERAGE(A5:C14,3,A5:C14)$$

A5:C14	Database list
3	The number of the field in the database that you are calculating
A5:C14	The entire database, since we do not have any criteria

OR

=DAVERAGE(A5:C14,C5,A5:C14)

A5:C14	Database list
C5	The address of the field you are calculating
A5:C14	The entire database, since we do not have any criteria

OR

=DAVERAGE(A5:C14,"Salary",A5:C14)

A5:C14	Database list
"Salary"	The name of the field that you are calculating
A5:C14	The entire database, since we do not have any criteria

3. Press the **Enter** key.

Example 2: Find the average salary of managers in the marketing department (Uses Criteria)
=DAVERAGE(database,field,criteria)

Our calculation field is salary. However if you do not yet have a criteria area defined, that will be your first step.

1. Copy the field headings to a blank area on the worksheet. Make sure to leave at least two blank rows beneath these headings. In our sample data on the previous page, I have placed the headings in row 1.

2. Type **Marketing** under the **Department** field name in the criteria area, and press the **Enter** key. The criteria area looks like this.

	A	B	C
1	**Department**	**Manager**	**Salary**
2	Marketing		

} *Criteria area*

3. Select the cell where you want your answer to appear.

4. Type any of the following formulas:
=DAVERAGE(A5:C14,3,A1:C2)

A5:C14	Database list
3	The number of the field in the database that you are calculating
A1:C2	The area in the worksheet where the criteria is defined

OR

=DAVERAGE(A5:C14,C5, A1:C2)

A5:C14	Database list
C5	The address of the field you are calculating
A1:C2	The area in the worksheet where the criteria is defined

OR

=DAVERAGE(A5:C14,"Salary", A1:C2)

A5:C14	Database list
"Salary"	The name of the field that you are calculating
A1:C2	The area in the worksheet where the criteria is defined

5. Press the **Enter** key.

As we go through the others refer to the notes used above if you have any questions about format. As a matter of fact you may wish to do that anyway to familiarize yourself with this procedure. The more comfortable you are, the more productive you will be later.

Counting - DCOUNT

Count the salaries of managers in the marketing department. (Uses Criteria).

=DCOUNT(database,field,criteria)

1. Set the criteria

	A	B	C
1	Department	Manager	Salary
2	Marketing		

} Criteria area

2. Select the cell where you will type your formula.
3. Type any of the following three formulas:
    =DCOUNT(A5:C14,C5,A1:C2)
    =DCOUNT(A5:C14,"Salary",A1:C2)
    =DCOUNT(A5:C14,"3",A1:C2).
4. Press **Enter.**

Example 3: Count the salaries of managers in the marketing department whose salary is greater than $90,000 (Uses Criteria, AND condition).

=DCOUNT(database,field,criteria)

1. Set the criteria.

	A	B	C
1	Department	Manager	Salary
2	Marketing		>90000

} Criteria area

2. Select the cell where you will type your formula.
3. Type any of the following three formulas:
    =DCOUNT(A5:C14,C5,A1:C2)
    =DCOUNT(A5:C14,"Salary",A1:C2)
    =DCOUNT(A5:C14,"3",A1:C2).
4. Press **Enter.**

 As you change the criteria, the cell containing your answers will automatically change. If you need to preserve your answer, but know that you are going to use the criteria over again, I recommend you follow this procedure:
1. Use the database function to calculate your answer.
2. Select the cell that has your answer.
3. Copy the cell.
4. Select a different cell where you want to preserve your answer.
5. Select **Edit>Paste Special>Values>OK**.

Maximum - DMAX
Example 4: Find the highest salary paid.
=DMAX(database,field,criteria)
1. Select the cell where you will type your formula.
2. Type any of the following three formulas:
=DMAX(A5:C14,C5, A5:C14)
=DCOUNT(A5:C14,"Salary", A5:C14)
=DCOUNT(A5:C14,"3", A5:C14).
3. Press **Enter**.

Example 5: Find the highest salary paid to managers in the marketing or research department. (Uses Criteria OR condition).
=DMAX(database,field,criteria)
1. Set the criteria.

	A	B	C
1	Department	Manager	Salary
2	Marketing		
3	Research		

} *Criteria area*

2. Select the cell where you will type your formula.
3. Type any of these three formulas:
=DMAX(A5:C15,C5,A1:C3)
=DMAX(A5:C15,"Salary",A1:C3)
=DMAX(A5:C15,3,A1:C3).

 Notice that the criteria area has changed to include row 3. The criteria area is now A1:C3.

4. Press the **Enter** key.

There are additional functions that you can use. See the chapter, *No More Mysteries About Formulas*, for more database formulas.

Summary

This has been an information packed chapter. Don't you agree? Excel provides so many options on methods of analyzing data, and I did not want to miss the opportunity to share them with you. The more you work with these features the more comfortable you will become. Try them on some of your data. You will be amazed how much you can find out about your data now that these methods of data analysis have been demonstrated.

Happy Analyzing!

Mail Merge Using Excel

*T*hose wonderful "personalized" letters that you receive indicating that you have won a fortune or pre-qualified for a three-day vacation, are simply form letters personalized through a database and a merging process. You can use this process to:

◆ Send letters to clients about a new offering which is too good to refuse.

◆ Notify family members about the upcoming reunion. (Mail Merge will help you to organize the reunion, mailings, directory, etc. even though it can't make family members respond on time.)

◆ Inform club members about a planning meeting.

◆ Et cetra.

This same feature makes it easy for you to:
◆ Create name badges.

◆ Produce mailing labels.

◆ Create an organization directory.

This chapter is not designed to deliver all the features of the mail merge process. It is intended, however, to make sure you know how to use Excel as your database when you use the mail merge feature.

CREATING FORM LETTERS WITH WORD AND EXCEL

A form letter consists of two parts.
1. Constant information – The letter
2. Variable information – The data in the spreadsheet

Since the process for Office 2000 is different from Office XP, we will look at both. These two procedures may look a little tedious, but they are straightforward.

Procedure — Office 2000

1. Create your letter leaving spaces within the document for information that will be inserted. Be sure to save it when you finish writing it.
2. Select **Tools>Mail Merge**.
3. Select **Create>Form Letters>Active Window**.

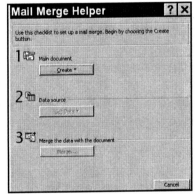

In the Mail Merger Helper dialog box you will find directions at the top to step you through the process

4. Select **Get Data>Open Data Source**.
5. Select the drop-down arrow in the **Files of type** box and choose **MS Excel Worksheets**.
6. Select the drive and folder that holds your file.
7. Click on the Excel file that you will use.
8. Place a check mark in **Select Method**.
9. Select **Open**.

10. Select **Microsoft Excel Worksheet via Converter** from the **Confirm Data Source** dialog box.
11. Select **OK**.
12. In the **Open Worksheet** dialog box, select the first **drop-down arrow** and choose the worksheet that contains your data. Click **OK**.
13. Click **Edit Main Document**.
14. Click the location in your document where you want to insert your first field. In the **Mail Merge** toolbar, you see the button to **Insert Merge Field**. Click this button to show the fields. Insert the fields that you want in the proper place in your document.

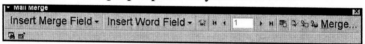

15. When all of the fields are inserted, select **Tools>Mail Merge>Merge>Merge**.

 There are many options available to you before you select your last Merge. You can sort records, select to merge only records that meet a criteria, merge directly to the printer, or merge to e-mail or fax.

Procedure Office XP

1. Create your letter leaving spaces within the document for information to be inserted. Be sure to save your document.
2. Select **Tools>Letters and Mailings>Mail Merge Wizard**.
3. From the **Mail Merge Task Pane** choose **Letters** (if you are creating labels or directories you would choose the appropriate one).
4. At the bottom of the task pane, choose **Next**.

5. At the top of the task pane, choose **Use the current document**.
6. Choose **Next: Select recipients**.
7. Choose **Use an existing list** from the top of the task pane. Then click **Browse** from the middle of the task pane.
8. Select the drive and folder that has your Excel worksheet. Choose your file. Choose **Open**.
9. Select your worksheet with the data on it. Click **OK**.
10. Select the recipients that will receive the letter. Click **OK**.
11. Click **Next: Write your letter**.
12. Click **Address Book** at the top of the task pane to determine how your letters are going to be addressed. Make your choice.
13. Click **Greeting Line** at the top of the task pane and select a greeting line.
14. Select the **More Items** icon on the task pane to see the fields to insert. This opens the **Insert Merge Fields** dialog box.
15. Position the cursor where you want the first field to be inserted into your letter.
16. Click **Insert**.
17. Close the dialog box.
18. Repeat the process of opening the **Insert Merge Fields** dialog box and inserting fields until you have all fields inserted.

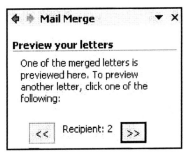

19. Click **Next: Preview your letters**.
20. Click the << to preview the previous letter, and >> to preview the next letter.

21. When you have finished previewing them, click **Next: Complete the merge**.
22. Click **Edit individual letters>OK**.

It is amazing how quickly you can produce hundreds and hundreds of letters using mail merge. This is one of the biggest times savers ever invented. Too many times I have entered offices and watch someone:

◆ Prepare a letter
◆ Print it
◆ Change the name and address
◆ Print it
◆ Change the name and address
◆ And continue this process until all of their letters are printed

Watching them go through this process just brings shivers to my spine. However, the person at the desk feels so good because they have found a way to avoid retyping the letter. If you know any one who is in this type of bondage – make a gift of this book to them. They will love you forever.

Don't forget that you can also create your name badges, mailing labels, directories (catalogs), and envelopes using mail merge. The process is very much like the one of creating form letters. Just remember when creating name badges, labels, tent cards, etc., you will need to select the label number and type. This will tell the system how big it is and prepare your text for correct placement.

Because of multiple requests it is very likely that I will document the tips and techniques for creating reports and labels using the mail merge process. If you think you would like to know about this why not send me a note and keep an eye on my web site.

Setting *Preferences* *in Excel*

*L*ike the rest of Microsoft Office, most of the preferences in Excel are set through the **Options** command.

EXCEL OPTIONS

1. Select **Tools>Options**.
2. Select the desired tab.
3. Choose your preferences.
4. Select **OK**.

You've heard the expression "If it's not broke, don't fix it." It's a worn out axiom, but it fits here, believe it or not. Thus, for the majority of the settings I recommend you leave them as they are (the default) unless you have a reason to change them. There are a few I will point out simply because they are the ones many of my clients seem to appreciate knowing about.

General Tab		
Selection	**Preference**	**Why?**
Recently used files	Increase the number of entries.	When you select **File** on the menu bar, the bottom of the commands list has the last four files used. Being able to click the name of the file opens it without your having to look for it. If you increase this number you will have more files listed at the bottom of the File menu, thus quickly available to you. I have mine set to seven or nine.
Sheets in new workbook	Set it to a number that is reasonable for your environment. I have mine set to "1".	It is so easy to add worksheets until I do not see the need to start each workbook with 3 blank sheets. Most of my workbooks only use one sheet anyway. If you normally use more sheets in your workbook, set this number to accommodate your needs. You can still add or delete sheets.
Standard Font	This sets the default font type and size for new workbooks.	Many clients tell me they do not like Arial size 11, which is the default formatting for new workbooks. If you want to use Times New Roman size 12 as the default whenever you start a new workbook, this is where you make the change.
User Name	Enter your name	When inserting comments and when tracking document changes this is where it will look to identify the user and place their name in the identification area.

Save Tab		
Selection	**Preference**	**Why?**
Save AutoRecovery info every XX minutes	The default of 10 minutes is fine unless you are in an area that experiences frequent power outages or if your system is experiencing problems.	This timing will determine how often an automatic saving of your files will occur. The longer the time period the more data you are likely to lose if there is a power outage or if your system freezes.

TOOLBAR OPTIONS

The other preference you may wish to consider is the appearance of your toolbars. You do want them to look their best, right?

◆ Should the standard and the formatting toolbars share the same row?

◆ Should all of your menu commands appear when you select the Menu name? Should the rest appear after a short delay?

◆ Or would you like to see all of the commands when you select the menu item?

These preferences are referred to as toolbar options. They are set through the **Customize** command.

1. Select **Tools>Customize**.
2. Select the **Options** tab.
3. Choose the desired options.
4. Select **OK**.

Each selection controls the appearance of some item in your toolbar.

1. Show standard and Formatting toolbars on two rows. If you want more of your toolbar icons to show on these two toolbars, place a check here. If you do not, the **Standard** and the **Formatting** toolbar will be on the same row next to each other. It will save space in your window, thus allowing more workspace, but will require you to click on the toolbar "show more buttons" icon to see the buttons that are hidden.

2. Always show full menus. This prevents showing a short list of menu commands when the menu item is selected. The entire list of commands will show. For Example, if **Always show full menus** is not checked, clicking **Format** will cause some of the commands listed under **Format** to appear. This list

is the "short menu." The bottom of the **Format** menu would show two arrows. Clicking on the two arrows, or waiting for a few seconds, would cause the rest of the commands under Format to appear.

3. Large icons. What an excellent feature for the sight-challenged over-forty crowd. Try it and see what I mean. Never again will you have to strain to see the toolbar buttons. Be aware that the number of toolbar buttons that will show will be limited. You will need to click the icon at the end of the toolbar to show the additional icons. But that is a small price to pay for seeing what you're working on.

4. List font names in their font. When you select the drop down arrow to select a font type you see a list of font names. If the **List font names in their font** box is checked the list shows up in the font type to show how the font will look. If this is not checked, you simply see a list – unformatted - and may have difficulty choosing which one you want.

5. Show screen tips on toolbar. This brings up a small yellow box when you rest on a toolbar button. This box will give a description of what function the toolbar button performs. This is a great little feature. It avoids your having to click an icon to find out what it does. The screen tip tells you in advance.

Toolbar options are a Microsoft Office setting – not an Excel one. The choices that you make will change the toolbar options for all of the office applications.

It is through the options and the customizing features that you communicate your preferences to Excel. Once you are more Excel comfortable, why not venture out and take a look at the other options available for you through the **Options** command.

Congratulations!

I hope you want to list this as one of your major "discovery" accomplishments. You have now earned an unofficial PhD in Excel. All your dedication, hard work, stretch breaks, and munchies attacks have paid off. As you become more familiar with Excel, you'll discover what a gold mine you have found in the procedure pages and in your own individualized study.

I don't know how many times you've exclaimed as you tapped your forehead with the palm of your hand: **"I Wish I Had Known That Yesterday!"** but I've got a feeling those words were accompanied with a sense of accomplishment.

Enjoy your new-found Excel knowledge. Take the time to broaden your skills. Look forward to many more palm taps on your forehead. I hope you will continue to excel in Excel. Now, put this book down and celebrate your success in Excelville. Keep it handy as a reference. Sleep with it under your pillow. (Remember that one from your school days?) Buy a copy for a friend. Let me know how many tips of value you picked up and how much time you think it will save you in the course of a week. I love giving out praises and yours is waiting for you.

Have a happy, healthy, productive Excel experience.

Notes

*H*as this been helpful? Did you pick up tips that would have been time savers if you had known them before? It is my hope that you have gathered some worth-while information, something that makes it easier and more enjoyable to use Microsoft Excel.

It may help to keep this list of notes handy for a quick reference.

Page #	Topic

Page #	Topic

Acknowledgements

It should be illegal to receive the amount of encouragement that my friends and my children give to me. How can I ever thank them for their messages of encouragement and their understanding when I take my laptop and go into hiding? I'm sure they know that when I re-surface, I will talk enough to catch up on everything that I missed.

Friends like Anna, Tressie, Lois, Earlene, and my BWIC sisters provided encouragement through their "You Go Girl!" cheers. The NC Career Technical Education teachers held my feet to the fire by letting me know that they were waiting and would be expecting to see this book by July 2004.

The title for this book came from the thousands of people I have had the pleasure of training. Their constant expression as I went through various classes and seminars was *"I Wish I Had Known That Yesterday!"* It is through their willingness to learn, that I have been able to teach. We share a mutual admiration.

As with all publications that have technical information, the amount of editing is unreal. Every formula and every function has to be tested. I could never, ever express to Twanda Baker, my daughter Tiffany, and dear friends Bernadette Johnson and Tressie Rooks, how much I appreciate the days and nights they spent editing and making recommendations when the wording wasn't crystal clear.

Only Sam Hunter, a gifted graphics artist, could find just the right shades of green for the cover, and not make a baby look like a little Martian. Thanks so much for the great job you did on designing the cover. Once again I called on Liberty Publishing to publish a book with an unbelievable schedule. Once again they met it with style. For this I will be forever grateful.

To those mentioned, and to the many unmentioned – Thank you! This could not happen without you.

Credits

For sure these procedures and functions included in this book are not solely the "brain children" of Lorraine Stephens. They are found in many references. Some of those references are *Microsoft®* publications, help screens, the web, newsletters, and books from various sources. My goal is to simplify them, make them easy to use, and put some of them into a handy reference guide such as this.

Many of the tips and techniques are gems that have been discovered simply through trial and error. Sometimes you just stumble up on an application secret that produces joyful results. Other times, your enthusiasm and common sense reinforce your building skills.

As always the main credit goes to you. You have taken the initiative to better your understanding of Microsoft Excel ®, to increase your productivity, and to better appreciate this application as a tool for capturing and analyzing data.

Congratulations!

 *About The Author*

Lorraine Stephens is President of L. Stephens and Associates, Inc., a Raleigh-based computer applications consulting firm. Over thirty-five years of experience in technical support, management, and training with major corporations, small businesses and school systems has earned her the reputation of being one of the most reputable computer application trainers and keynote presenters in the business. She assists companies and individuals to *learn without fear*, maximizing their productivity through effective use of computer applications. Among her well-received programs are her feature keynote, *Tackle Technology and Win*, and her popular *"I Wish I Had Known That Yesterday!"* series, of which this book is a part.

In addition to specific applications, she offers keynotes, end user seminars and personal training on Laptop Productivity. As an expert in her field she has received her Microsoft Office User Specialist (MOUS) certification, and is a certified MOUS Master Instructor.

With a commitment to community, Lorraine currently serves as a member of the Disciplinary Hearing Commission of the North Carolina State Bar Association, and on the Executive Board of the YWCA of the Greater Triangle Area.

Her professional and service organizations include The American Business Women's Association, Raleigh Professional Women's Forum, Chamber Executive Women's Task Force, Delta Sigma Theta Sorority, Inc., The National Speakers Association, Black Women's Investment Club, Inc., and Toastmasters International.

She has two wonderful children, a son, Dorrian and a daughter, Tiffany, both of whom are educators.

Also by Lorraine G. Stephens:
"I Wish I Had Known That Yesterday!" – *MICROSOFT WORD:*
Increasing Your Productivity & Enhancing Your Documents

For more information on Lorraine Stephens'
workshops, seminars and presentations
or
To order additional copies of this book, contact:

L. Stephens & Associates, Inc.
The Education and Technology Group
6325-9 Falls of Neuse Road
PMB 322
Raleigh, NC 27615-6809
Office: (919) 876-3100
Fax: (919) 877-0189
e-mail: Lorraine@Lorrainestephens.com